THE
GREATEST
PUZZLES
EVER SOLVED

This edition published by Metro Books,
by arrangement with Carlton Books Limited

Copyright © 2009 Carlton Books Limited

ISBN 978-1-4351-2111-9

Printed and bound in China

10 9 8 7 6 5 4 3 2 1

THE GREATEST PUZZLES EVER SOLVED

200 enigmas that have challenged mankind, from the dawn of time to the present day

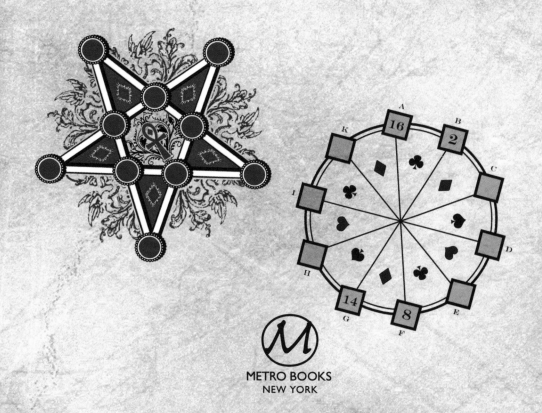

METRO BOOKS
NEW YORK

CONTENTS

INTRODUCTION

Puzzles are one of the areas of human experience that transcend all cultural barriers. Every nation on Earth has puzzles, and probably has done for as long as humankind has been able to reason. Faced with the unknown, our natural curiosity drives us to find some sort of resolution. When we know that the mystery has been set in front of us as a test, the urge to solve it – to prove ourselves – becomes almost unbearable.

Deduction is probably mankind's single greatest tool. The ability to reason and theorize – to connect cause and effect into a model of the world – has led us from the early caves to our current society of wonders. Without it, there would be no technological progress, no real understanding of others, no written language... no humanity. Our capacity for logical reasoning is the main quality that separates us from the rest of the animals. So perhaps it's no surprise that we all get enjoyment from exercising that ability.

Puzzles give us the chance to exercise our mental muscles. That is not just a metaphor; in many important senses, it is a literal description of the way our minds work. Push your mind's limits, and your brainpower will get stronger, more flexible, faster – fitter. Ignore it, and it will get weaker and flabbier, exactly the same way that a body does. Recent scientific discoveries have shown that the brain really does respond to mental exercise, and solving puzzles can even help to stave off the effects of diseases like Alzheimer's.

The parallels between physical and mental exercise run deeper, too. Like physical exercise, mental exercise gives us a sense of achievement, improves our mood, and can give us a lot of pleasure. Achievement in puzzle solving and logical thought can even be a mark of status, similar to that of an athlete. In China and Japan, mental agility has been regarded as a highly skilled competitive sport for centuries, with some of the top stars becoming household names.

A Historical Overview of Puzzling

Just as puzzles can be found in all corners of the world, they can also be found in the archaeological records of all the ancient cultures for which we have substantial remains. Puzzles are as widespread in time as they are in space. The oldest mathematical devices that we have found so far are actually earlier than the oldest true writing we've discovered. The devices are a set of carvings in the form of the so-called Platonic Solids, dated around 2700BC. Each is a three-dimensional shape made from a number of identical regular polygonal 2-D shapes. There are only six Platonic Solids, of which the cube is by far the best known. As the carvings obviously lack any written notes, we don't know for sure how they were used, but it's certainly telling that they pre-date written language so far.

The earliest puzzle definitely identified so far originated in ancient Babylonia, and dates to around 2000BC. It involves working out the lengths of the sides of a triangle. From them on, the preserved record of our puzzle activity gets steadily stronger. The Rhind Papyrus is an ancient Egyptian riddle that is thought to come from much the same sort of time. A few hundred years later, Phoenician puzzle jugs – which required some lateral thinking to fill and drink from – became popular. By 1200BC, dice had been invented. This innovation occurred during the long, dull siege of Troy if the legends are to be believed.

A well-documented craze for lateral thinking and logical deduction puzzles and riddles swept through ancient Greece from the 5th century BC, lasting for several hundred years. That carried on over into ancient Rome in the form of advanced mathematical and logical work. The Chinese invented Magic Square puzzles around 100BC, calling them "Lo Shu", river maps. Other Chinese puzzle advances followed, including the first sets of interlocking puzzle rings around 300AD, the game of Snakes and Ladders by 700AD, and the first versions of playing cards in 969AD, with a deck of cards made for the Emperor Mu-Tsung. These had little in common with modern playing cards, however. The deck of cards we know now almost certainly came from Persia some hundred years later, arriving into Europe with Spanish sailors.

The traditional puzzle game of Fox and Hounds arose in the 12th century in Scandinavia. Despite persistent rumours of great antiquity, Tangrams – one of the most famous Chinese puzzles – remain unknown before 1727AD, making them a comparatively recent innovation. From the 19th century onwards, as the global economy slowly started to take genuine shape, puzzles became a significant business, and they proliferated worldwide. Some of the most currently famous include the game Tic-Tac-Toe, which was invented in 1820 by the father of modern computing, Charles Babbage, and Lucas' Towers of Hanoi puzzle from 1883. It was the crossword, created in 1913 by Arthur Wynne, that really took over the world however – even Rubik's Cube from 1974 and Howard Garns' Sudoku from 1979 haven't had the same impact. New puzzles keep coming all the time though, and the one thing you can be sure of is that the next world-beater is somewhere around the corner.

Tim Dedopulos, dedopulos@gmail.com

THE ISHANGO BONE

The Ishango tribe lived in Zaire in Africa around 9000BC, and may have been amongst the forefathers of modern African people. Out of all the many archaeological discoveries that have been made regarding the Ishango, perhaps the most significant is a small tool, made out of a bone handle with a chunk of quartz set into the end. It's thought that the Ishango Bone was used for inscription of some sort – perhaps engraving, maybe even writing. That alone would make it fascinating. But the Ishango Bone contains three sets of numbers, in the forms of columns of scratches marked into its sides. Although there remains some academic uncertainty, it is thought that each of the three groups represents a depiction of the tribe's knowledge of mathematical processes – astonishing, given the era. The first column is the plainest. There is a 3 next to a 6, a 4 next to an 8, and a 10 next to a 5, along with a further 5 and a 7. Leaving aside the last pair for the moment, these pairs clearly indicate multiplication by two.

What mathematical processes do the other two sides indicate, and where do the remaining 5 and 7 from the first side fit?

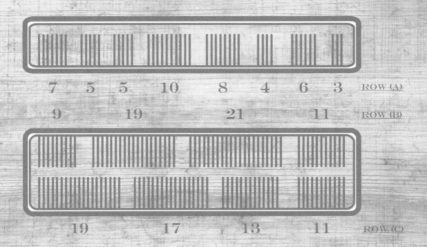

| 7 | 5 | 5 | 10 | 8 | 4 | 6 | 3 | ROW (A) |
| 9 | | 19 | | 21 | | 11 | | ROW (B) |

| 19 | 17 | 13 | 11 | ROW (C) |

ZAIRE
9000BC

SEE ANSWER 1

Holy Days

The ancient Egyptian cult of Isis began some time before 2500BC, and survived into ancient Greece and Rome. Isis was the goddess of fertility and motherhood, and her husband, Osiris, was the god of the underworld. Lunar symbolism was central to the cult, which believed that Osiris had been murdered and dismembered, before being (mostly) put back together by Isis, who then resurrected him.

Members of the cult of Isis believed that Osiris had been killed on the 17th of the lunar month, the point at which the moon's waning becomes obvious. As a result, that day – and number – was abominable, ritually taboo. By contrast, 28, the length of the lunar month, was sacred, and Osiris was said to have reigned (or sometimes lived) for 28 years. Osiris was even said to have been chopped into 14 parts, representing the 14 days of the moon's waning.

The cult also held two other numbers in esteem however – the only two possible whole-number perimeter values of a rectangle which encloses the same area as its own length. Which two numbers are they, and why else might they have been important to the cult?

EGYPT
2000BC

SEE ANSWER 2

FRUSTRUM

The Moscow Papyrus is the oldest known Egyptian mathematical text. It is thought to date to some time shortly before 2000BC, making it somewhat older than its longer, more detailed cousin, the *Rhind Papyrus*. *The Moscow Papyrus* was purchased, contents unknown, by Egyptologist Vladimir Goleniscev around the end of the 19th century, and then re-sold to the Pushkin Museum in 1909. The scribe responsible for the Moscow Papyrus did not record his name, but the manuscript is also sometimes known as the *Goleniscev Mathematical Papyrus*. Problem 14 of the *Moscow Papyrus* poses this unusually sophisticated question:

If you are told that a truncated square-base pyramid has 6 for the vertical height, by 4 on the base and by 2 on the top, what is the volume?

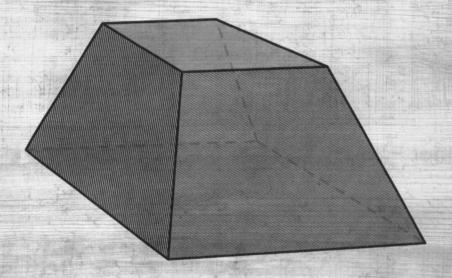

EGYPT
1950BC

SEE ANSWER 3

TRIANGLES OF BABYLON

This puzzle is taken from a Babylonian clay tablet dating from around 1900BC, found in the Schøyen Collection – a wonderful treasury of philanthropically-assembled manuscripts of all types from the last five millennia – and gives an interesting geometric problem. It is thought that the tablet might have been something in the nature of an assignment for students, because it doesn't give the answer to the problem.

As you can see in the image, two equilateral triangles are nested in one another, parallel on all sides. The smaller has a side length of three; the larger, 5. What is the area of the space between the two triangles?

SEE ANSWER 4

Ahmes' Loaves

The oldest remaining collection of puzzles known to us is a collection of mathematical problems from ancient Egypt. It was written in 1650BC by a scribe named Ahmes, working from now-lost parchments that were at least 200 years older, and may have even dated from times before that. The collection is known as the *Rhind Papyrus*, after the Scotsman who bought the document, as an Egyptian curio, in the 1850s. The *Rhind Papyrus* provides us with an invaluable insight into Egyptian mathematical techniques and logical thought. One of the more interesting peculiarities of the Egyptian system was their method of subdividing whole numbers. They understood the idea of fractions, to a sophisticated degree, but did not have any conception of fractional multiples. In other words, they understood the idea of ¼ easily, but the idea of ¾ was totally alien. In fact, even the idea of repeating the same fraction for one given number would have confused them. So if an ancient Egyptian subtracted ¼ from 1, he would not have thought of the remainder as ¾, or even as ¼ + ¼ + ¼, but as ½ + ¼.

Bearing that in mind, one of Ahmes' puzzles asks the reader to divide three loaves of bread between five men. What solution would he have understood? It will help if you think about the problem practically – each man must receive not only the same amount of bread, but also the same type and number of pieces, each of which must be a different size.

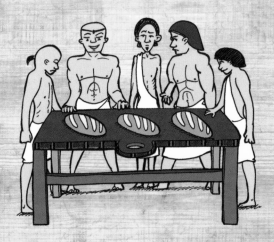

EGYPT
C. 1850BC

SEE ANSWER 5

As I was going to Amenemhet III's

The best-known puzzle in the *Rhind Papyrus* is famous primarily because it has survived down through the centuries, travelling via Rome to end up in 18th century Europe and on to the modern era. The Rhind version barely bothers to give the question, concentrating instead on the answer, presumably because the question was already so well-known. Everything considered, it has aged remarkably well.

A wealthy priest owns seven houses. Each of these houses contains seven cats. Each cat must eat seven mice, because each mouse can eat seven sheaves of wheat. A sheaf of wheat can produce seven hekats of grain. Houses, cats, mice, sheaves, grain: how many in total fall within the priest's domain?

A QUESTION OF QUANTITY

In Problem 24 of the *Rhind Papyrus*, Ahmes asks the reader to calculate a missing quantity:

One amount added to a quarter of that amount becomes 15. What is the amount?

EGYPT
1850BC

SEE ANSWER 7

A Fractional Issue

Ahmes presents a number of problems in the *Rhind Papyrus* that are clearly meant to give instruction and practice with the issue of doubling any given unit fraction. As $^2/_3$ was the only allowed fraction that wasn't 1/#, and repeating a fraction within a single number wasn't allowed, this was a somewhat thorny issue. Ahmes presented a table of fractions and their doubles – $^1/_5$, for example, doubled to $^1/_3 + ^1/_{15}$ – but we have modern techniques instead.

Problem 21 of the *Rhind Papyrus* asks the reader to complete $^2/_3 + ^1/_{15}$ to 1. Can you do it following the Egyptian rules?

EGYPT
1850BC

SEE ANSWER 8

Strong Grain

Ahmes sets this puzzle involving equivalent values in Problem 72 of the *Rhind Papyrus*. We can quickly recognize that the problem is one of percentages, but that was not a concept that fitted readily with the Egyptian mathematical system.

A group of men have 100 hekats of barley of impurity (pesu) 10. They wish to exchange it for a fair quantity of inferior barley, of pesu 45. What is the fair quantity?

EGYPT
1850BC

SEE ANSWER 9

Progressive Loaves

The mathematical rule of *Regula Falsi* (or False Position) states that, when attempting to solve a mathematical problem, if you put in a value that you know to give the wrong answer, the proportion of the wrong answer to the answer you want should indicate the proportion by which your initial value is incorrect. As a very trivial example, look at the question x*3 = 6. Try x=1, and you get 1*3 = 3. You need to double 3 to get 6, so you need to double 1 to get the right answer, 2. Obvious here, but more useful when the question is complex, although you might need to try two or three progressive possibilities to see a clear trend.

In the *Rhind Papyrus*, Ahmes lists a question that, at the time at least, required quite sophisticated use of the *Regula Falsi* in order to be solved.

100 loaves are to be divided unevenly between five men. The amount of bread received by each man decreases by the same amount each time, and the last two men's shares together are equal to just ¹/₇ of the first three's collected shares. By how much do the shares decrease each time?

Egypt
1850BC

SEE ANSWER 10

DATES

Some of the questions in the *Rhind Papyrus* can get quite complex, particularly given the mathematics of the time. For some, the key really does lie in finding the best available technique for cracking the nut of the problem, rather than settling for a less ideal method of solution.

Bear Egyptian mathematical peculiarities in mind as you consider Problem 28 of the Papyrus. A quantity together with its two-thirds has one third of its sum taken away to yield 10. What is the quantity?

EGYPT
1850BC

SEE ANSWER 11

THE RULE OF THREE

The 24th puzzle of the *Rhind Papyrus* provides an interesting example of a problem and solution technique that would go on to become fundamentally important to businesses in the Middle Ages. It was even known as The Golden Rule for a time, because of its significance to mercantile trade.

As Ahmes puts it, "A heap and its $\frac{1}{7}$th part become 19. What is the heap?"

EGYPT
C. 1850BC

SEE ANSWER 12

PROGRESSIVE SHARES

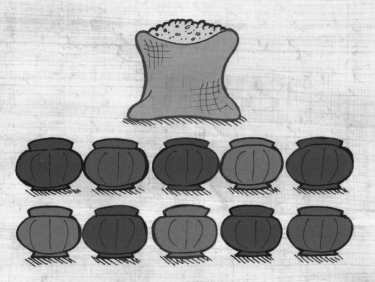

One of Ahmes' more challenging trials involves a rather complex question of mathematical progression – the sort of thing which at one point was thought to have first emerged with the great Greek mathematicians.

In Problem 64 of the *Rhind Papyrus*, he asks:

If it is said to you to divide 10 hekats of barley amongst 10 men, so that the difference of each man to his neighbour in hekats of barley is ⅛th of a hekat, then what is each man's share?

You may make do with finding just the largest share, to save calculating a lot of Egyptian fractions.

EGYPT
C. 1850BC

SEE ANSWER 13

SQUARING THE CIRCLE

This is one of the *Rhind Papyrus*'s more important puzzles, indicating the understanding of pi as a mathematical constant. Ahmes didn't have an accurate value for pi, but he was clearly aware that there was one, and that it was absolutely fundamental to geometry.

In this puzzle, there is a cylindrical granary of diameter 9 and height 6. How much grain can go into it?

The question assumes that the reader doesn't have any knowledge of pi, so when you're answering this one, you're not allowed to use the standard formula for the area of a circle. Can you work out the answer from first principles?

**EGYPT
C. 1850BC**

SEE ANSWER 14

SQUARE TRIAL

The *Berlin Papyrus* is another ancient Egyptian scroll, one that contains a mixture of medical and mathematical information. It has the earliest known information on pregnancy testing, and is generally classified amongst the Egyptian medical papyri rather than the mathematical ones. It was found early in the 19th century at Saqqara, and like the *Moscow Papyrus*, it is anonymous. It also contains one of the most sophisticated Egyptian *Regula Falsi* problems still extant today.

An area of 100 square cubits is equal to that of two smaller squares together. The side of one is ½ + ¼ the side of the other. What are their sides?

EGYPT
C. 1800BC

SEE ANSWER 15

SUMERIAN RIDDLE

Sumer, in what is now southern Iraq, is regarded as the cradle of civilization. The nation arose as humans started deliberate intensive cultivation some seven to eight thousand years ago, and the availability of stored food allowed people to move beyond just hunting and gathering to performing social roles that did not directly provide food or defence. Complex records were required to keep all this running, and writing grew out of it as a direct result.

This riddle dates from the last phase of Sumerian history; Sumer would eventually fall, largely thanks to the ecological results of its farming enterprises, to be replaced by Babylon.

There is a house. One enters it blind. One leaves it seeing. What is it?

SUMER
1600BC

SEE ANSWER 16

RAMESSES' STAR

Pharaoh Ramesses II ruled Ancient Egypt at the height of its glory, and had an immense impact on the kingdom. His grandest architectural work was his memorial temple, the Ramesseum at Kurna. It remained an important centre of learning and worship for centuries after his death. The temple was found by modern European scientists at the end of the 18th century. Among the hieroglyphs and decorations, they discovered a curious puzzle painted onto a ceiling – Ramesses' Star. It is one of the oldest puzzles known, and may have been the forerunner of the medieval game of Nine Men's Morris.

The aim is to fill nine of the ten circles on the star with coins, beads, or anything else handy. Place a coin on any empty circle on the star, and jump it over one circle (empty or filled) to another empty circle in a straight line. It is possible to fill nine of the ten circles this way, but it is not easy – if you find yourself getting stuck at six or seven circles, then persevere, and try some lateral thinking.

EGYPT
1213 BC

SEE ANSWER 17

THE RIDDLE OF THE SPHINX

The Riddle of the Sphinx is probably the most famous and enduring riddle of them all.

The Sphinx was a monster of ancient Greek myth, the daughter of Typhon and Echidna, with the body of a lion, the head and chest of a woman, a snake in place of a tail, and the wings of an eagle. Although she hailed originally from Ethiopia, she waited in the hills outside the city of Thebes, and demanded that travellers answer her riddle. When they failed to do so correctly, she devoured them. Her question was: "Which creature goes on four legs in the morning, two at mid-day and three in the evening, and the more legs it has, the weaker it is?"

GREECE
C. 800BC

SEE ANSWER 18

THE QUIET ONE

This is another ancient Greek riddle that has survived since antiquity. As is often the case, it is the universal themes that remain enduring.

What has a mouth but does not speak, what has a bed but never sleeps?

GREECE
C. 700BC

SEE ANSWER 19

Visitors

This simple riddle dates back to ancient Greece, and has survived through to the modern day:

At night they come without being called.
By day they are lost without ever leaving.
Who are they?

GREECE
c.600BC

SEE ANSWER 20

CRETANS

Epimenides of Knossos was a Cretan Greek poet, philosopher and visionary in the 6th century BC. In his poem Cretica, he rails against his fellow Cretans for denying the immortality of the god Zeus, saying "The Cretans, always liars, evil beasts". At some point, the poem became associated with the liar paradox, and eventually became known as Epimenides' Paradox.

There is no one formulation of the paradox, but put simply, it says that Epimenides, a Cretan, says "All Cretans are liars." But he himself is a Cretan. If he is telling the truth, his statement has to be a lie, and he is not telling the truth; if he is lying, then he is giving weight to the truth of his statement, and therefore not lying.

What flaws are there in this?

GREECE
C. 550BC

SEE ANSWER 21

ZENO'S DICHOTOMY

Zeno of Elea was a Greek philosopher who lived from around 490BC to around 430BC, and was placed into a large mortar and pounded to death after taking part in an unsuccessful attempt to overthrow the tyrant Demylus. He was a member of the Eleatic School of philosophy, which held that all existence and time is but one construct, and all appearances to the contrary – plurality, motion, change and so on – are illusory. As a young man, he wrote a book of forty logical paradoxes to support the Eleatic philosophy and bolster his master, Parmenides. Zeno hadn't even decided whether to publish the book or not when it was stolen and published without his permission, and eight of his paradoxes survive, thanks to commentaries by Aristotle and Simplicius. Today, they are his most famous legacy.

In this Dichotomy, also known as Zeno's Racecourse, he points out that movement is impossible because any movement must pass through the half-way stage before it arrives at its goal. But then the half-way stage becomes a new goal, and it too has a half-way, and so on. In fact, even the tiniest movement has an infinity of ever-smaller half-way stages that must be reached first, and no finite amount of time is enough to reach an infinite number of stages.

Ignoring the fact that this is a *reductio ad absurdum* argument that is experimentally obviously wrong – things move – is there a logical flaw here?

GREECE
C. 470BC

SEE ANSWER 22

ZENO'S ARROW

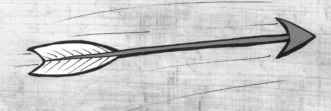

In the Paradox of the Arrow, Zeno points out that an arrow occupies a specific area of space when it is at rest. He then points out that in any given instant, the arrow in flight is at rest. If, during one tiny instant of time, the arrow moved, then it would be possible to divide the instant into before and after moments. Therefore the arrow is motionless, and therefore motion has to be an illusion or, at the very least, to occur between moments somehow, outside of time.

Was he wrong?

GREECE
C. 470BC

SEE ANSWER 23

ZENO'S STADIUM

Another of Zeno's paradoxes of motion is that of the stadium. Imagine that there are two lines of five runners, A and B, running around a track in opposite directions. They are moving at the same speed, as can be clearly observed by a row of five stationary spectators, C. Each row of people is the same length. The two rows of runners cross as they are passing the spectators, A on the outside. The length of A is the same as the length of B and C, and A and B are moving at the same speed. The first member of A will run the entire length of B in x seconds. But B, running at the same speed, will only run half the length of C in the same time. As the lengths of B and C are the same, Zeno asserts that time is $x = x*2$, which is impossible, and therefore time is illusory.

Is there anything to Zeno's argument?

GREECE
C. 470BC

SEE ANSWER 24

Achilles and the Tortoise

Zeno's most famous paradox is that of Achilles and the Tortoise. In it, he gives a situation where Achilles is in a race with a tortoise, and gives the tortoise a 100m head-start. Once the tortoise reaches 100m, Achilles races to catch up with it. But in the time taken to do so, the tortoise has moved further on. Achilles must catch up to the new point – by which time the tortoise will have moved again. In fact, Achilles will never be able to catch up, because the tortoise will always have moved on by the time he gets to where it had been.

Where's the problem?

GREECE
c. 470BC

SEE ANSWER 25

THE HEAP

The Sorites Paradox, named after the Greek word for heap, was coined by Eubulides of Miletus, a Megarian (or Eristic) philosopher from the 4th century BC who spent much of his energy bitterly attacking Aristotle, who was his contemporary. Megarian philosophy, founded by Euclid of Megara, espoused the idea of a single, perfect goodness, a state of grace with similarities to Zeno's Eleatic unity.

Eubulides is known for his paradoxes, most of which arise from setting up situations with vague starting conditions. The Sorites paradox states that a large number of grains of sand collected together is a heap, and taking one grain of sand from it does not stop it being a heap. So is it still a heap when only one grain of sand remains? And if not, when did it switch to not being a heap any more?

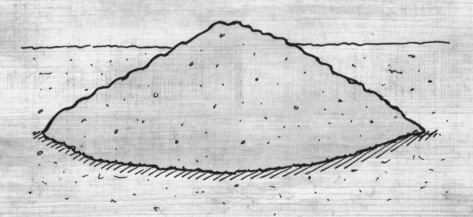

GREECE
C. 440BC

SEE ANSWER 26

FOUR BROTHERS

This riddle reflects interestingly on ancient Greek thought.

There are four brothers, in this world, who were all born together.
The first brother runs and runs, and never grows tired.
The second brother eats and eats, and is never full.
The third brother drinks and drinks, and is never sated.
The fourth brother sings an unending song, and it is never good.

GREECE
C. 400BC

SEE ANSWER 27

THE SHOOT

This short but puzzling riddle comes from ancient Greece:

What has roots that nobody sees,
and towers taller than the trees.
Up, up and up it goes,
Yet day by day it never grows.

GREECE
c. 400BC

SEE ANSWER 28

THE NURSERY

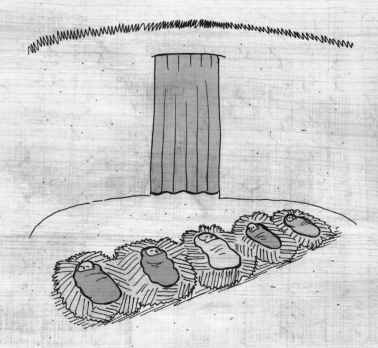

This ancient Greek riddle can still stretch modern ingenuity:

There was a green house.
Inside the green house was a white house.
Inside the white house was a red house.
Inside the red house, lots of babies.

GREECE
C. 400BC

SEE ANSWER 29

THE LUO RIVER SCROLL

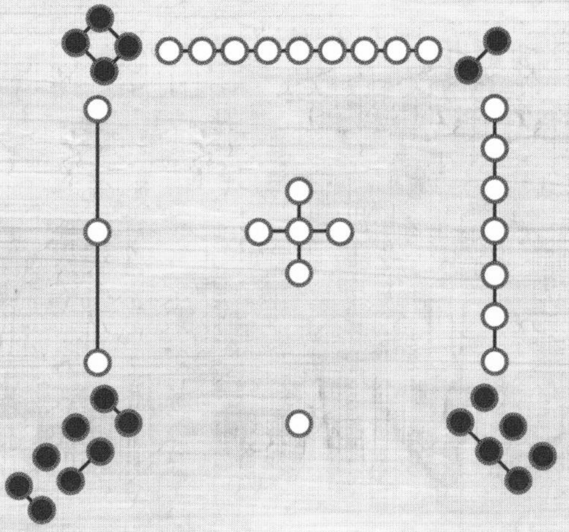

According to legend, China's first emperor was Fu Hsi, half man and half dragon, who consolidated the country into one kingdom around 3000BC. As he was riding along beside the Ho Tu, the Yellow River, one day, he saw a dragon-horse rise from the water, and on it was a curious design, a series of dots set in concentric rings and linked in a particular arrangement. This pattern became known as the Yellow River map, and from it, Fu Hsi derived the eight trigrams of Chinese mystical thought that form the famous divination system of the I Ching, the Book of Changes.

Almost a thousand years later, the Emperor Yu – another legendary figure – was riding beside the Lo Shu, the Luo River, when a tortoise rose from the water, bearing markings similar to the Yellow River map, but in a very different pattern. This pattern became known as the Lo Shu, the Luo River scroll. Yu used it to re-order the eight trigrams, linking them to the five Chinese elements, and it was said that Fu Hsi's arrangement represented the order of things before the world was created, whilst Yu's arrangement represented the order of things in the physical world.

The Lo Shu, shown above, has been captivating and enthralling people all over the world ever since its discovery, although modern scholars put that at around 400BC rather than 2300BC. How is it better known in the West?

CHINA
c. 400BC

SEE ANSWER 30

BURIDAN'S ASS

In *De Caelo* (*About the Heavens*), Aristotle discussed the theoretical possibility of a man who is equally hungry and thirsty being poised, equidistant, between food and drink. Unable to decide, he moves to neither, and eventually dies.

French philosopher Jean Buridan, a 14th century thinker, became associated with the problem because he suggested that any fully-informed human when faced with alternative options will always choose the one that leads to the greatest good, after due consideration. Later philosophers used Aristotle's thoughts to satirise Buridan, suggesting that an ass placed between two equally tempting bales of hay would starve trying to decide which to eat.

One common response to the paradox is to point out that sometimes an arbitrary decision is perfectly rational, and that it is much more rational just to pick one rather than starve. Can you think of another response?

GREECE
340BC

SEE ANSWER 31

Hui Shi's Third Paradox

The Chinese philosopher Hui Shi lived some time around the start of the 3rd century BC, during China's Warring States period. He was famous as a rhetorician, devoting himself to a doctrine that argued the arbitrary nature of human perception, and the consequent need to treat all of nature benevolently. He left a set of ten famous paradoxes, some of which are not so much paradoxical as statements of philosophy.

In Hui Shi's third paradox, he states that "Heaven is as low as earth, mountains are level with marshes."

What is he getting at?

CHINA
C. 300BC

SEE ANSWER 32

THE ZERO PROOF

There are a number of places where common mathematical assumptions break down, and provide scope for seemingly paradoxical proofs. Euclid collected together an entire volume of such falsities, to help show the importance of rigour in mathematical thought. It is reasonably straightforward to show that $0 = 1$, and by extension, that maths is flawed.

Start by adding an infinite number of zeros together. No matter how much nothing you add, you still have nothing. $0 = 0 + 0 + 0 + 0 + 0 +...$

Now, $1 - 1$ is 0, so you can just as easily read that as $0 = (1 - 1) + (1 - 1) + (1 - 1) +...$

But if that is true – and it is – the associative law states that you can bracket the sums as you like, so long as you don't change the order of any digits, so $0 = 1 (-1 + 1) + (-1 + 1) + (-1 + 1) +...$

As $(-1 + 1)$ is 0, this becomes $0 = 1 + 0 + 0 + 0 +...$

And $0 = 1$.

What's the error?

GREECE
C. 300BC

SEE ANSWER 33

CROCODILE TEARS

An ancient Greek paradox of uncertain authorship involved a hungry crocodile snatching a baby from its mother on the banks of the Nile. The mother begged for mercy, and the crocodile wanted to look good in the eyes of the gods, and so agreed to give her a chance to win her baby back. The crocodile told her, "If you correctly predict the fate of your baby, then I will return him. Otherwise, I will eat him."

Given that the crocodile wants to eat the baby, is there anything that the mother can say to get her child back?

GREECE
C. 300BC

SEE ANSWER 34

THE LADDER OF HORUS

The right-angled triangle has been one of the most prevalent and fundamental mathematical discoveries in human history. It allows the reliable construction of square angles, which in turn permits advances in construction, manufacturing and a host of other areas. The most common version found in history is the poster-boy for Pythagoras' theorem, the 3-4-5 triangle.

The Egyptians had early knowledge of the importance of right-angled triangles, with particular emphasis on the 3-4-5. It was said that the length 3 section belonged to Isis, the length 4 section to Osiris, and the length 5 hypotenuse to their son, the hawk-headed god Horus.

The earliest clear use of the triangle as an Egyptian puzzle appears around 300BC. The problem it asks is trivial to us, of course: "If a ladder of 10 cubits has its base 6 cubits from a wall, how high will it reach?" The answer is a simple doubling of the Pythagorean triple of 3-4-5.

A more interesting question is about Pythagorean triples themselves, which consist of three integers that could describe the sides of a right-angled triangle. Discounting any simple multiples of other triples, how many triples are there with a hypotenuse of less than 20?

EGYPT
C. 300BC

SEE ANSWER 35

THE SIEVE OF ERATOSTHENES

Prime numbers, being indivisible, are one of the most fundamental mathematical concepts, and, like square numbers, have often been the source of mystical speculation. The ancient Greeks were particularly sophisticated in their handling of prime numbers. The Greek mathematical master Euclid proved that there must be an infinite number of primes.

You can use Euclid's method to discover new primes, with patience, but you can't be sure of catching all of them that way. You can also use even more patience and, for each number, check if it can be divided by the other primes you already know to discover if it is prime. If you get past its square root without finding a prime divisor, your target number is prime. You'll get them all, but while that's OK for small numbers, it's horribly time-consuming for larger ones.

Eratosthenes, an approximate contemporary of Euclid's from the 3rd century BC, devised a brilliantly simple way of making it quicker to find prime numbers, and it became known as his Sieve, for the patterns it made. Given the technique's name, can you work out what the method is?

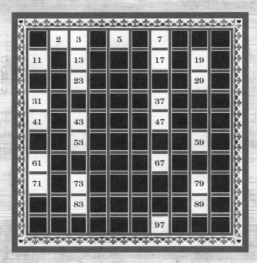

GREECE
C. 250BC

SEE ANSWER 36

Archimedes' Revenge

Archimedes of Syracuse was a Greek scientist who died in 212 BC at the age of 75. He is remembered as one of the greatest mathematicians of all time, and possibly the greatest scientist of the ancient world. It is said that he devised the most fiendishly difficult puzzle of all, created as a challenge and rebuke to Apollonius of Perga, a geometrician who had suggested improvements to some of Archimedes' theorems. Archimedes' Revenge was then supposedly sent to Eratosthenes, the chief librarian at the legendary Great Library of Alexandria, for the library staff to work on.

The challenge is to calculate the numbers of the cattle of the sun, belonging to the gods. There were four different herds, one white, one black, one yellow and one dappled. The number of white bulls was equal to a half plus a third of the black bulls, plus all of the yellow bulls. The black bulls were equal to a quarter of the dappled plus a fifth, plus all of the yellow ones. The dappled bulls were equal to one sixth of the white plus one seventh, plus all the yellow ones. The number of white cows was equal to one third plus a quarter of the entire black herd. The black cows were equal to a quarter of the dappled herd plus a fifth. A quarter of the dappled cows were equal to a fifth plus a sixth of the yellow herd. The yellow cows were equal to a sixth plus a seventh of the white herd. When the white and black herds mingled, their combined number was a perfect square. Similarly, when the dappled and yellow herds mingled, they came to a triangular number. How many cows and bulls were there in each herd?

Be warned: many professional mathematicians would need either a high-powered computer or several years of hard work to solve this puzzle.

GREECE
C. 230BC

SEE ANSWER 37

THE NINE CHAPTERS

The Nine Chapters on the Mathematical Art is a collection of mathematical teachings from early China. The book was known in 179AD, and may actually be several centuries earlier; its most important commentary, written in 263AD by mathematician Liu Hui, credits Zhang Cang, who died in 142BC, as the work's earliest compiler. The actual original authors are anonymous, but the book illuminated and shaped mathematical thought in the East until at least the 1600s.

One of the book's most important concepts is that of abstract numeration. Concrete numeration is obvious to anyone – one apple is one apple, both three grapes and three plums are groups of 3, and so on. The natural numbers are just that, natural. Abstract numbers are far harder to grasp if you don't already know them. The *Nine Chapters* contains problems which require the use of both 0 and negative numbers to solve. Both of these are extremely counter-intuitive, and require that you think of absence as somehow a concrete, solid thing.

This puzzle is from the eighth chapter, "Fang Cheng".

There are three grades of corn, each of which comes in a basket of a particular size. Two baskets of first-grade corn do not make one measure, and neither do three baskets of second-grade corn, nor four baskets of third-grade corn. However, if you add one basket of second-grade to the two first-grade baskets, or one basket of third-grade to the three second-grade baskets, or one basket of first-grade to the four third-grade baskets, then you would have one measure in each case. What proportion of a measure does each basket size contain?

CHINA
C. 150BC

SEE ANSWER 38

THE CISTERN PROBLEM

The cistern problem dates back to the *Nine Chapters*, and is part of a common thread of puzzle challenges that crops up regularly in civilisations all over the world. This is probably because the premise is both practical and fairly fundamental.

There is a cistern of volume 48 which has two inlet taps and one outlet tap. The first inlet tap alone will fill the cistern in 12 hours. The second alone will fill it in 6 hours. The third alone will empty it in 8 hours. If the cistern is emptied and all three taps are opened, how many hours will it take for it to fill up?

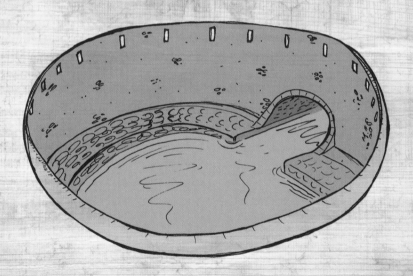

CHINA
C. 150BC

SEE ANSWER 39

DOG AND HARE

The sixth chapter of the *The Nine Chapters on the Mathematical Art* deals with the mathematical knowledge required for purposes of taxation – how to distribute taxes, transport grain, and so on. This section also introduced pursuit problems, where the puzzle involves working out how soon a pursuing party will catch up with a fleeing one. The possible implications of this inclusion are left to the reader.

    This puzzle states that a fleeing hare and a chasing dog are 50pu apart. The dog will catch the hare after a chase of 125pu. How much longer will the chase be once the dog has closed to a distance of 30pu?

CHINA
C. 150BC

SEE ANSWER 40

THE CHICKENS

The seventh chapter of the *The Nine Chapters on the Mathematical Art* is devoted to what the authors called 'Excess and Deficiency' problems – the same sort of *Regula Falsi* approach that Ahmes made use of in the *Rhind Papyrus*. In the Chinese method, two answers were usually given, one greater and one lesser than the actual answer required, which is where the technique drew its name from.

In this puzzle, a group of people are buying a consignment of chickens from a stall, and they are each paying the same amount of money. If they each contribute 9 wen, they are paying 11 wen too much, and if they contribute 6 wen, then are paying 16 too little.

How many people are there, and what is the cost of the consignment?

CHINA
c. 150BC

SEE ANSWER 41

LEG AND THIGH

The entire ninth chapter of *The Nine Chapters on the Mathematical Art* is about right-angled triangles, possibly because they were so critical in accurately assessing land distribution for farming. The chapter is named Kou Ku, a term derived from the names given to the sides of a right-angled triangle. The two sides that formed the right-angle on a right-angled triangle were named Kou and Ku, Leg and Thigh. The hypotenuse, stretching between the two tips, was known as the Hsien, or lute-string.

This puzzle is concerned with discovering the size of the largest square that can fit inside a right-angle triangle, making use of the pre-existing right-angle in its construction.

There is a right-angled triangle with Kou of 5 ch'ih, and Ku of 12 ch'ih. How many ch'ih is the largest square that can fit inside?

CHINA
C. 150BC

SEE ANSWER 42

MEN BUY A HORSE

The *Nine Chapters* also features the first known instance of the Men Buy a Horse puzzle, a commonly-encountered type of problem.

There are three men who are considering buying a horse that costs 24 yuan. Individually, none of the three has enough money. The first man says, "If I borrowed a half of the money that you two have, I could buy the horse." The second man says, "If I borrowed two thirds of the money that you two have, I could buy the horse and still have around half a yuan left." The third man says, "Well, if I borrowed three quarters of the money that you two have, I could buy the horse and still have one and a half yuan left over."

Assuming each man has a whole number of yuan, how much does each man have?

CHINA
C. 150BC

SEE ANSWER 43

Greed

This Ancient Greek puzzle is somewhat more abstract than it appears at first blush:

The more of them you take for yourself, the more of them you leave behind for others. What are they?

GREECE
C. 100BC

SEE ANSWER 44

Posthumous Twins

The Posthumous Twins problem arose when Roman law decreed that the legal heir of an estate should receive at least 1/4 of that estate, and if the will was invalidated, only the deceased's children could inherit. The idea was to cement the rights of the eldest son of the deceased with respect to a possible widow or other claimant.

In this problem, a dying man with a pregnant wife makes a will which states that if his wife has a male child, the son should get ⅔ of the estate and the wife should get ⅓. If she has a female child, the wife will get the larger ⅔ share, and the daughter will get ⅓. After the man's death, the wife gives birth to twins, one boy and one girl.

How is the estate to be shared?

Rome
c. 50BC

SEE ANSWER 45

THE SHIP OF THESEUS

Plutarch was a Greek-born philosopher and historian who lived in the 1st century AD. He is best known now for his book *Parallel Lives*, a series of 23 biographical studies of historical figures, arranged in pairs, one Greek, one Roman. He looked at character, in particular, and drew interesting correspondences between his pairs.

In a piece on the Greek hero Theseus, Plutarch notes that on his return to Athens, the ship that he had travelled in was preserved as a historic relic. As the planks decayed, the old timbers were removed, and replaced with lovingly-crafted exact duplicates. In this manner, the ship was preserved down through the centuries, even to the 3rd century BC.

The question Plutarch poses is, if all of the pieces of wood that make up the ship have been replaced, possibly many times, is it still the same ship?

ROME
c. 100AD

SEE ANSWER 46

MEN FIND A PURSE

The Men Find a Purse problem has been cropping up regularly in different mathematically-inclined cultures since its first appearance in ancient Greece. In his masterwork *Liber Abaci*, published in 1202, Fibonacci devotes an entire section of the book to discussion of the problem and various different versions of it.

Three men were walking together when they discovered a purse of money. They examine the purse, and the first says to the second, "If I took this purse, I would have twice as much money as you." The second says to the third, "I would have three times as much as you." The third says to the first "I would have four times as much as you." How much does the purse hold, and how much does each man have?

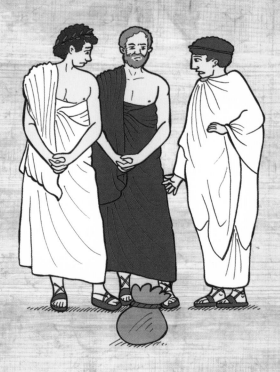

GREECE
250AD

SEE ANSWER 47

THE UNWANTED

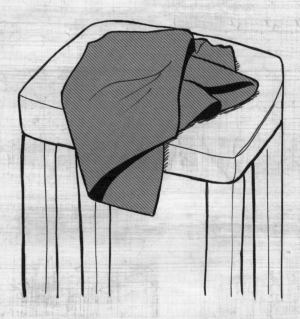

This is a rather telling riddle from Roman times:

He who has it does not say it.
He who takes it does not know it.
He who knows it does not want it.
Yet, men die for it.
What is it?

ROME
c. 300AD

SEE ANSWER 48

THE FIVE SONS

It was an Arabic puzzle which took the idea of even distribution of varied resources to a pinnacle of complex challenge. Its history is uncertain, but it appeared in several volumes of Arabic puzzle collections in the second half of the last millennium, and may have been considerably older than that.

 In this puzzle, a dying father leaves a range of wine casks to his five sons. His bequest amounts to 45 casks in total, 9 holding 4 pints, 9 holding 3 pints, 9 holding 2 pints, 9 holding 1 pint, and 9 containing nothing. The wine is to be shared equally, in both amount of wine (18 pints) and number of casks (9). Each son wants to get at least one of each cask, and each of them wants to receive a different distribution of casks to any of their brothers.

 How can this be done?

ARABIA
c. 400AD

SEE ANSWER 49

SUN TZU'S CLASSIC PROBLEM

In the book *Sun Tzu Suanjing*, 3rd century AD Chinese mathematician Sun Tzu – a different person to the world-famous military general, who lived some five centuries earlier – introduced an important principle in number theory, known now as the Chinese Remainder Theorem. His illustrative question for the Theorem has become known as Sun Tzu's Classic Problem.

We have a group of things of which we do not know the number. If we count them by threes, the remainder is two. If we count them by fives, the remainder is 3. If we count them by sevens, the remainder is two. How many things are there?

CHINA
c. 400AD

SEE ANSWER 50

THE TROUBLE WITH CAMELS

A traditional Arabic puzzle, most likely owing its conception to the ancient Egyptian style of fractional representation, specifies that in an old Arabian city, a wealthy merchant died and, in his will, left specific instructions regarding the disposition of his livestock. His lawyer met the merchant's three sons, and explained to them that his father had insisted that his eldest son receive a full half of his camels. The middle son was to get a third of the herd, and his youngest son, still with plenty of time to make his fortunes, was to get just one ninth.

Unfortunately, the herd consisted of 17 camels, and the brothers could see no way to honour their father's wishes without killing at least one of the beasts and chopping it into chunks. The lawyer, however, had a better idea. Without any loss to himself, and without involving a fifth party, he was able to show the brothers how the herd could be divided equally, keeping all the camels alive.

How did he do it?

ARABIA
C. 400AD

SEE ANSWER 51

THE SNAIL AND THE WELL

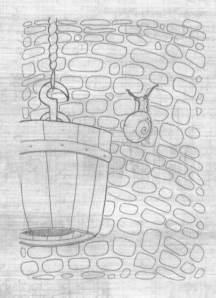

The Snail and the Well puzzle first appeared in India, with the great Jain mathematicians. Its earliest appearance dates to some time after the work of the celebrated 7th century mathematicians Bhaskara and Brahmagupta.

A snail is at the bottom of a well 4½ feet deep. On the first day it climbs two feet, and then slips back down one foot during the night. It is getting tired however, and so each subsequent day, it climbs 10% less that it did the day before. It always slips down the same one foot at night. Will the snail ever get out of the well, and if so, when?

INDIA
c. 700AD

SEE ANSWER 52

ALCUIN'S CAMEL

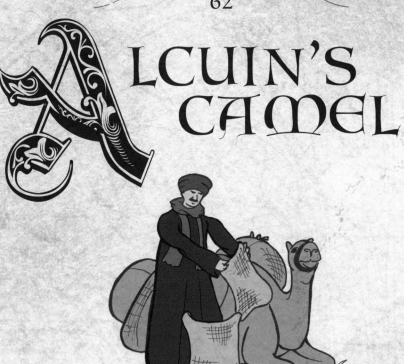

Alcuin of York was a religious scholar and teacher in Dark Age Europe. He was a student at the great school of York, which was founded in 627AD by St. Paulinus of York. The school, now called St. Peter's, is the world's fifth-oldest school. Some time around 750 AD, Alcuin assumed a teaching role at the school, and became headmaster in 767 AD. As well as the obvious religious studies, the school taught the liberal arts and sciences, which included logic and mathematical subjects.

Alcuin of York is thought to be the author of the *Propositiones ad Acuendes Juvenes* (*Propositions for Sharpening Youths*), one of the first books of puzzles collected for teaching or recreation. The oldest surviving copy dates to the end of the 9th century.

One of Alcuin of York's better known puzzles from the *Propositiones* is an early example of what is now known as the jeep problem. A certain head of a household ordered that 90 modia of grain be taken from one of his houses to another, 30 leagues away. Given that this load must be carried in three trips (the camel can manage 30 modia as a maximum load), and that the camel must eat one modius per league, how many modia can be left over at the end of the journey?

England
770AD

SEE ANSWER 53

Brothers and Sisters

Several of Alcuin of York's problems remain popular and influential today in one form or another. Possibly the best known of these is this puzzle, where three brother and sister pairs need to get across a river in a small boat, but to stop the men's lust overcoming them, a woman may only be in the presence of a man if he is her brother, or if her brother is present.

There were three men, each having an unmarried sister, who needed to cross a river. Each man was desirous of his friends' sisters. Coming to the river, they found only a small boat in which only two persons could cross at a time. Let them say, they who are able, how did they cross the river, so that none of the sisters were defiled by the men?

Given the dubious assumption that all men would be happy to rape their friends' sisters given a moment's chance, the best solution takes 11 crossings.

What is the process?

ALCUIN'S FLASKS

In this puzzle, Proposition 12, Alcuin of York describes a situation where flasks containing three different volumes of oil are to be divided equally among three sons so that each gets the same.

A father dies and leaves his three sons 30 flasks. 10 of these are full of oil, 10 are half-full, and 10 are empty. Divide the oil and flasks so that an equal share of both comes to each son.

All well and good. But is it possible to do this so that each son gets a different distribution of flasks to the other two, and each son gets at least one of each type of flask?

England
770AD

SEE ANSWER 55

The Eastern Merchant

Another of Alcuin of York's problems asks the reader to solve a problem of indeterminacy. A certain merchant in the East wished to buy 100 assorted animals for 100 solidi. He ordered his servant to pay five solidi per camel, one solidus per ass, and one solidus per 20 sheep, and to get at least one of each. Let them say, they who wish, how many camels, asses and sheep were obtained for 100 solidi?

England
770AD

SEE ANSWER 56

ALCUIN'S GRAIN

This is Proposition 32, Concerning the Head of a Certain Household. Alcuin of York gives a distribution problem as a way of encouraging his students to work around issues of indeterminate conditions. He actually gives several such problems, varying mainly in the amount of grain, which rather reinforces that he wanted the students to learn the knack of solving problems of this sort.

A head of a certain household has 20 servants. He ordered them to be given 20 modia of corn as follows: the men should receive 3 modia, the women 2 modia, and the children, half a modium. Let them say, they who can, how many men, women and children must there have been.

You should assume that there is at least one of each.

SEE ANSWER 57

The Hundred Steps

Alcuin of York's 42nd Proposition, Concerning the Ladder Having 100 Steps, was famously given to a young Johann Gauss, a German scientist who remains known as one of the most influential mathematical figures in history. Gauss was only seven at the time, which dates the event to 1784 AD. It is said that by the time the teacher had finished instructing the class in the problem, Gauss had the solution.

There is a ladder which has 100 steps. One dove sat on the first step, two doves on the second, three on the third, four on the fourth, five on the fifth, and so on up to the hundredth step. How many doves were there in all?

England
770AD

SEE ANSWER 58

ALCUIN'S RIDDLE

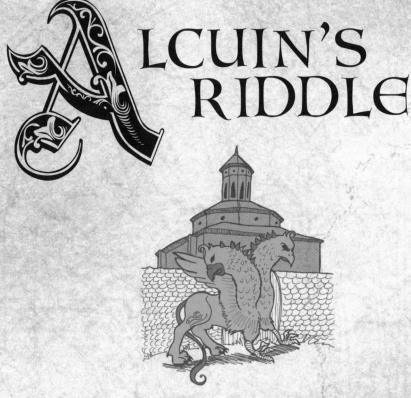

In 781AD, Alcuin was reluctantly poached away from York by the Emperor Charlemagne, to revitalise the school at his court. In this latter role, he educated many of Europe's leading nobles, scholars and ecclesiasts, training them in the liberal arts and sciences, and becoming friendly with most of them.

Alcuin posed the following riddle to the Archbishop Ridulf of Mainz, known as Damoeta, in return for a gift:

> A beast has sudden come to this my house,
> A beast of wonder, who two heads has got,
> And yet the beast has only one jaw-bone.
> Twice three times ten of horrid teeth it has.
> Its food grows always on this body of mine,
> Not flesh, fruit. It eats not with its teeth,
> Drinks not. Its open mouth shows no decay.
> Tell me, Damoeta dear, what beast is this?

Ridulf had the advantage of knowing what gift he had just sent Alcuin. Can you identify the 'beast' without that inside knowledge?

England
c. 780AD

SEE ANSWER 59

The Josephus Problem

Titus Flavius Josephus was a Jewish war-leader during the first Jewish-Roman war, 66–73AD. He was captured by the Romans in 67AD, and persuaded to work as a negotiator for them. He documented the fall of Jerusalem in 70AD, and became a Roman historian shortly afterwards.

During his capture, Josephus says that he found himself trapped in a cave with 40 companions. The Romans asked him to surrender, but his men refused to allow it, opting instead for collective suicide. They formed a circle and killed each other one by one, killing the third man each time and closing the circle's ranks. By claimed happenstance, Josephus was in the correct place to be the last man alive, and he persuaded the man before him, the second to last, to surrender with him.

This historical event became the object of mathematical speculation, first appearing as a puzzle in an Irish text from around 800AD. If Josephus started in position number 31 in the circle of 41, where would his surviving compatriot have been?

Ireland
c. 800AD

SEE ANSWER 60

The EXPLORER'S PROBLEM

The original version of The Explorer's Problem originates with Alcuin, and his camels, in the 8th century AD. This problem departs somewhat from Alcuin's original question, but provides an interesting counterpoint to it.

An explorer in the desert wishes to arrive at an oasis as darkness is falling, so that he does not have to sit around in the heat, nor will he risk missing the oasis in the darkness. From his current position, if he rides at 10 miles an hour, he will arrive an hour after darkness has fallen. If he rides at 15 miles an hour, he will arrive an hour too soon, and swelter. At what speed should he ride to reach the oasis at sunset?

United Kingdom
c. 800

SEE ANSWER 61

ONKEY NUTS

A highly influential 9th century Indian mathematician, Mahaveeracharya, established the impossibility of discovering the square root of a negative number, described a method for discovering lowest common multiples, made several key advances in geometry, and disentangled mathematics and astrology, setting the ground for Indian mathematics – already sophisticated – to develop even further.

In his 850AD treatise *Ganit Saar Sangraha*, the *Mathematical Digest*, Mahaveera posed this question which still regularly appears in puzzle compendiums and newspaper entertainment pages today.

Three sailors and their pet monkey find themselves shipwrecked on a small desert island. They immediately set to gathering a pile of coconuts, and when darkness falls, they decide to divide the coconuts in the morning. During the night however, one sailor awakes and decides to take his third early. He divides the pile into threes, with one coconut left over, which he gives to the monkey. He then hides his third, and piles the remaining coconuts back together again. Later, another sailor awakes and does exactly the same, again finding that when he divides the pile into three, there is one coconut left to give to the monkey. Finally the third sailor follows suit, again with one coconut left for the monkey. In the morning, the sailors awake, and agreeably divide the pile of coconuts remaining into three. Once more, there is one left over, which they give to the monkey.

What is the least number of coconuts that there could have been to begin with?

India
c. 850AD

SEE ANSWER 62

The BOOK OF PRECIOUS Things

Abu Kamil, an Egyptian mathematician who lived between 850 and 930AD, was a dedicated algebraist who earned himself the nickname al-Hasib al-Misri, "the Egyptian Calculator". In his *Book of Precious Things in the Art of Reckoning*, he laments the fact that many puzzles have multiple possible answers, and people tend not to realize this. He gives the example of this puzzle, which proves to have far more answers than generally recognized.

It is a reasonably straightforward indeterminate problem: you must buy 100 birds using exactly 100 drachmas. Ducks cost 2 drachmas each, Hens are 1 drachma, a dove is ½ drachma, a ringdove is ⅓ drachma, and a lark is ¼ drachma. You need to buy at least one of each. How many of each do you buy?

It's not too tricky to get an answer for. If you want a real challenge though, also work out how many possible solutions there are.

SEE ANSWER 63

 A MEDIEVAL RIDDLE

Leofric, the first bishop of Exeter, assumed his lofty position in 1050AD. Among other acts, he donated a large book of poems and riddles to the cathedral library. The *Exeter Book*, as it is now known, is the largest surviving collection of Old English literature. The author or compiler is unknown, but the date of its creation is thought to have been in the second half of the 10th century. Riddle 25 of the *Exeter Book* has become well-known. See what you make of it.

"I am a wondrous creature: to women a thing of desire; to neighbours serviceable. I harm no city-dweller, except my slayer alone. My stalk is erect and tall – I stand up in bed – and shaggy down below (I won't say where). Sometimes a countryman's comely daughter will venture, proud girl, to get a grip on me. She assaults my redness, plunders my head, and fixes me in a tight place. The one who afflicts me so, this woman with curly locks, will soon feel the effect of her encounter with me – an eye will be wet."

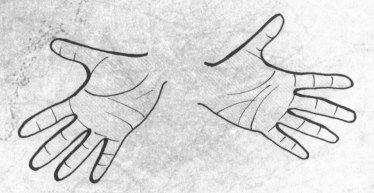

England
c. 950AD

SEE ANSWER 64

The Mariner

This interesting riddle is found in the *Exeter Book*, Leofric's gift to Exeter Cathedral library on his assumption in 1050AD.

> Often I must war with waves, fight the wind –
> Strive with both at the same time – when I depart to seek
> the earth beneath the waters. To me, my home is alien.
> If I am strong in the struggle, if I can hold my ground.
> Should I fall back, even a little, my foes are stronger,
> and, wrenching me away, soon force me to flee,
> stealing away the treasure that I must keep safe.
> I will forbid this so long as my tail endures,
> and the stones have power against my strength.
> What am I called?

England
950AD

SEE ANSWER 65

The Memory Wheel

The images shown here are simple examples of memory wheels, used in such disparate settings as Sanskrit poetry, telegraph communication, probability theory and even some older computing applications. In fact, the larger of the two wheels is intrinsically linked to the Sanskrit sutra "YamAtArAjabhAnasalagAm", which is first thought to have appeared around 1000AD.

How are the wheels used, and how do they link to the YamAtArAjabhAnasalagAm?

India
c. 1000AD

SEE ANSWER 66

JIA XIAN'S TRIANGLE

Travelling mathematics teacher Zhu Shijie was one of the greatest Chinese mathematicians of the middle ages era. Two of his books have made it through to modern times, the 1299AD *Introduction to Computational Studies*, and 1303's *Jade Mirror of the Four Unknowns*. The former work was an introductory textbook on maths, algebra and geometry that shaped mathematical development in the region for centuries. The *Jade Mirror* was significantly more important however, pushing back the boundaries of algebraic thought at the time.

Amongst the other techniques and innovations in the *Jade Mirror*, Shijie documented a mathematical tool known as Jia Xian's Triangle, used to solve complex polynomial equations. The Triangle dated back to around 1050AD, first appearing in a work called *Shi Suo Suan Shu* by the mathematician Jia Xian. The Triangle predates several important European mathematical discoveries, and its first discovery may have been as early as 500BC in India.

How is it derived and, in the West, better known?

China
c. 1050AD

SEE ANSWER 67

The Old One

Riddles have been an important part of oral cultures worldwide for centuries. Try this one:

Though I'm of great age,
I'm held in a cage,
And have a long tail and one ear.
My mouth it is round,
And when joys abound,
Oh, then I sing beautiful clear.

United Kingdom
c. 1200AD

SEE ANSWER 68

The Trouble with Rabbits

This is a simple, well-known puzzle, but it has its genesis in 13th century Italy, and its implications have been profound for both mathematics and the natural sciences.

Assume that there is a pair of mature rabbits at a certain place, entirely surrounded by a wall. The nature of these rabbits is such that they breed another pair every month, and that the newcomers themselves reach maturity and begin to breed in the second month after their birth.

How many pairs of rabbits can be bred from this pair in one year?

Italy
1202AD

SEE ANSWER 69

The Ring Game

In 1202, Leonardo of Pisa introduced the Hindu-Arabic number system to Europe in his book *Liber Abaci*, the *Book of Calculation*. Fibonacci, as he is now usually known, travelled around southern Europe and north Africa studying with the greatest Arab mathematicians of the time, and became one of the greatest mathematical minds of the Middle Ages.

Liber Abaci explained the decimal system, gave clear instructions on multiplication and fractions, and showed how the Hindu-Arabic system related to the full range of commercial transactions – and, more to the point, how it made them much simpler than with Roman numerals. It had a huge effect on European thought, and paved the way for the Renaissance, and the growth of European culture

In the *Liber Abaci*, Fibonacci describes a game which mathematically adept hosts can use to impress and confound their guests. The guests sit in a line, and one of them chooses a ring he or she is wearing. This person takes their position in the line, doubles it, adds 5, multiplies by 5, and then adds 10 to this total. Then the number of the ring-finger across the two hands is counted and added, and the value is multiplied by 10. Finally, a number for the knuckle joint is added on. Obviously, both hosts and guests have to agree on the numbering in advance! "When this number is announced," as Fibonacci says, "it is easy to pinpoint the ring."

How?

SEE ANSWER 70

The Well

In the *Liber Abaci*, Fibonacci introduced the Well Between Two Towers problem:
There are two towers, the heights of which are 40 paces and 30 paces. They are 50 paces apart, and between the two towers is a well. Two birds, sitting atop the two separate towers, take wing at the same instant, and fly at the same speed directly to the well. They arrive there at the same time. What distance is the well from the higher tower?

Italy
1202AD

SEE ANSWER 71

TARTAGLIA'S WINE

Niccolo Fontana was a 16th century Venetian mathematician and engineer. He became known as Tartaglia, "The Stammerer", after receiving a savage wound to his mouth and tongue during the French massacre of his birth-town of Brescia. He was just twelve. Essentially self-taught, Tartaglia went on to publish a host of books, including very important translations of Euclid and Archimedes.

In his works, Tartaglia published a measuring puzzle that first appeared in the writings of the Abbot of the Convent of the Blessed Virgin Mary, in Stade, near Hamburg, around 1240. The puzzle remains well-known and popular today.

You have three jugs which can hold 8, 5 and 3 pints of wine respectively. The largest one is full, and the other two are empty. Without spilling any wine, or using any other tools, it is possible to end up with two equal four-pint portions.

How?

Germany
c. 1240AD

SEE ANSWER 72

Topsy-Turvy

This traditional English riddle looks simple until you think about it:

What is·it that walks all day on its head?

England
c. 1300AD

SEE ANSWER 73

The Wanderer

This traditional English riddle has been around since the medieval period at least:

> Old Mother Twitchett had just one eye,
> And a dangling tail which she let fly.
> Every time she leaped over a gap,
> She caught a bit of her tail in a trap.

England
c. 1400AD

SEE ANSWER 74

The hound

An interesting traditional riddle from medieval Germany:

I run through woods and fields all day,
Sit under the bed at night in company,
With my long tongue hanging out,
Waiting only to be fed.

Germany
c. 1450AD

SEE ANSWER 75

EGIOMONTANUS ANGLE

The 15th century German astrologer and mathematician Regiomontanus was a celebrated scholar even in his own lifetime. He was said to have fashioned an eagle made of wood which was able to fly from the city under its own power, meet and salute the emperor, and return again. His interest in astrology and astronomy gave him great insight into trigonometric mathematics, and Copernicus considered him an influential inspiration. Regiomontanus' angle problem was devised to reinforce certain geometric principles.

Suppose there is a painting hanging from a wall, its base above eye level. If one stands too far away, the painting appears small. If one stands too close, it is foreshortened. In fact, there is just one point at which the viewer gets the maximum exposure to the painting, the place which maximises the angle formed between the top of the frame, the viewer's eyes and the bottom of the frame.

Where is it?

Germany
c. 1460AD

SEE ANSWER 76

The Problem of Points

The issue of the Problem of Points dates to a hypothetical situation posited by Fra. Luca Pacioli, an Italian mathematician and priest, in 1494. Pacioli described a game in which two players were competing. Each had an equal chance of winning any given round, and agreed in advance that the overall winner of X many rounds would collect the prize.

But what happens if the game is interrupted before it is finished? How could the players divide the pot fairly, taking into account the state of play at the time?

Italy
1494AD

SEE ANSWER 77

Modesty

English tradition has this riddle to offer:

> I am within as white as snow,
> Without as green as herbs that grow;
> I am higher than a house,
> and yet am lesser than a mouse.

England
c.1500AD

SEE ANSWER 78

 DURER'S SQUARE

Albrecht Dürer, who died in 1528 aged 56, was an artist at the centre of the Renaissance in Europe, and was instrumental in helping its spread into Germany and the rest of northern Europe. He helped establish woodcuts as an art form, was one of the first landscape painters, and produced vitally important works on artistic theory.

One of Dürer's greatest works is an allegorical engraving titled *Melencolia I*. The piece is laden with symbolism and hidden meaning, and remains one of the most hotly-debated and analysed prints today. In *Melencolia I*, a most incredible Magic Square hangs on the wall behind the main figure. In it, the rows, columns and diagonals all add to 34, and the two numbers at bottom centre are also the date of the engraving, 1514. There are a number of surprising symmetries if you square all the numbers too, and more besides than we have scope to discuss here.

Consider just the number of different ways that this square can be divided into four groups of four numbers, using all the numbers in the square just once, so that each of the groups sums to 34. How many are there – including rows, columns and diagonals/off-diagonals?

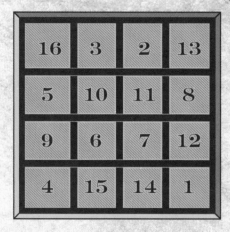

Germany
1514AD

SEE ANSWER 79

AN ODD GIFT

This medieval Spanish riddle poses an interesting intellectual challenge.

It is yours. You create it. You give it to another, who treasures it and holds it close. You keep it still, as you value yourself.

What is it?

Spain
c. 1525AD

SEE ANSWER 80

LOCK STRIKING PROBLEM

German mathematician Christoff Rudolff of Augsburg was the first European to draw attention to the Chinese use of decimal notation in maths, in 1530AD, and he also coined the use of the square root symbol, possibly as a stylised 'r' from the Latin word for a square root, 'radix'. He was also the first person to pose the Clock Striking Problem:

How many times does a clock's chime strike between noon and midnight? You may assume that the clock strikes only the hour, that it is 12-hour rather than 24-hour, and that the times are inclusive.

Germany
1526AD

SEE ANSWER 81

The Dinner Party

This is a puzzle from 16th century Germany, and provides an interesting example of linear indeterminacy, harking back to an 5th century Hindu problem.

A group of 41 people – men, women and children – have been dining at an inn. Their bill comes to 40 groschen, and they divide this up so that each man is paying 3 groschen, each woman is paying 2 groschen, and each child is paying ⅓ groschen.

How many men, women and children made up the group of 41?

Germany
c. 1540AD

SEE ANSWER 82

Tricking the Landlord

This is an interesting variant of the Josephus problem that surfaced in medieval Austria, and gained enough popularity to spread through Europe.

It is said that an inn landlord hosts a dinner for 21 friends and family. Being all reasonably well to do, they agree that one member of the group will pay the whole bill for the evening. That person is to be decided by fortune. When the time comes to leave, the landlord's barman will start somewhere in the group and then start counting them in a clockwise direction, with every seventh person counted free to leave the table. When there is but one left, he will pay for the evening.

The barman, however, holds something of a grudge against his master. He decides to make sure that it is his boss who ends up footing the bill. Where does he need to start his count?

ROUND AND ROUND

The Sun King, Louis XIV, is remembered as the ruler who oversaw the heights of the French monarchy's trend towards luxury and self-indulgence. His father, Louis XIII, was the king whom the Cardinal de Richlieu served as prime minister, at the time of the setting of Dumas' *The Three Musketeers*. This riddle dates from that period, although admittedly it is slightly more modest in nature than some of the excesses of the time.

What goes around the house and into the house without ever touching the house?

BACHET'S SCALES

French mathematician Claude Bachet is probably best known for his translation of the book *Arithmetic* by the Greek scholar Diophantus, partly because it was a marginal note in a copy of this volume that revealed the world-famous mathematical problem of Fermat's Last Theorem. But Bachet's work was important in its own right too, and he made important contributions in number theory and other areas.

In 1612, at the age of 31, Bachet produced a book of mathematical puzzles and curiosities, *Problemes Plaisants*. He re-issued it in 1624, in a revised and expanded form. In the larger *Problemes*, he posed this interesting challenge:

If you have a pair of scales, what is the smallest number of weights required to measure the weight of any other object that has an integral weight of between 1 and 40?

France
1624AD

SEE ANSWER 85

RUPERT'S CUBE

Prince Rupert, Duke of Bavaria was the younger son of a Bavarian noble house in the 17th century. He was at various times a soldier, a pirate, an artist, an inventor and a businessman, rising to considerable levels of achievement in several of those areas. He eventually financed the creation of the Hudson Bay Company, and was its first director.

Imagine a cube with a hole cut through it that leaves the cube in one single piece. Do you imagine that the largest cube able to pass through such a hole would be larger, the same size or smaller than the cube with the hole cut into it?

The Newton-Pepys Problem

In 1693, famous English public servant and diarist Samuel Pepys entered into correspondence with Isaac Newton, the father of physics. The topic under discussion related to a wager that Pepys was considering. Pepys wanted to know which of three dice rolls had the greatest odds of success. These were to roll six dice and get at least one 6, to roll twelve dice and get at least two 6s, and to roll eighteen dice and get at least three 6s.

Which is more likely?

England
1693AD

SEE ANSWER 87

Sunday

This riddle was popular in Germany at the end of the 17th century.

There were five men travelling to the church one Sunday. The heavens opened, and it started to rain. The four men who went for cover all got wet. The one man who did not move remained dry. How?

The TOURIST

This is one of the more enigmatic of the traditional riddles. It may take some ingenuity to crack.

I journeyed to the city.
I stopped there.
I never went there.
I came back again.

Switzerland
c. 1700AD

SEE ANSWER 89

The Bridges of Konigsberg

Königsberg was founded in 1255AD by crusader knights as a base of operations, and swiftly grew in importance to become the capital of East Prussia, finally being incorporated into the German Empire in 1871. It was taken over by the USSR in 1945, and is now the Russian city of Kaliningrad.

The Prussian city of Königsberg straddled the river Pregel, and there were two large, built-up islands in the river connected to each other and the two banks by a set of bridges. It became a matter of near-legendary dispute amongst locals (and visitors) as to whether it was possible to walk through the city crossing each bridge, as shown below, once and only once.

The Swiss mathematician Leonhard Euler finally proved in 1736 that it was impossible. What was his reasoning?

As an aside, it may be interesting to know that one of the bridges was rebuilt in 1935, two were destroyed in World War II and not rebuilt, and two more were replaced with a linked piece of highway after the war. So there are now five bridges, only two of which are antique. A Euler walk is now possible though, albeit one that begins on one island and ends on the other.

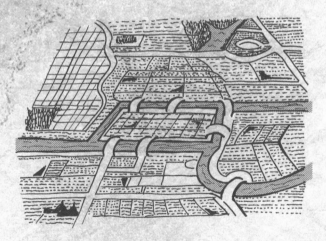

Prussia
1736AD

SEE ANSWER 90

 ALKING THE WALK

Starting from point A in the graph below, it is possible to travel along every line in the graph exactly once. Can you find such a route? This puzzle follows on from Euler's work with the Bridges of Königsberg (see previous page) to pose a rather tangled problem.

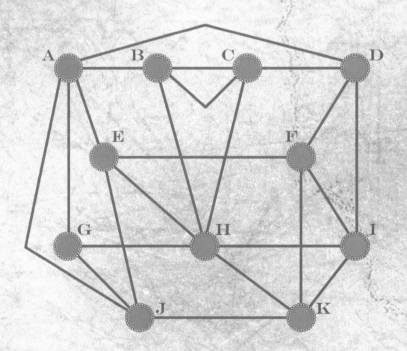

Switzerland
1736AD

SEE ANSWER 91

The Tethered Goat

This problem first surfaced in the pages of a society digest, presumably as a practical query from a livestock owner.

Imagine you have a circular field. You want to tie the goat to the fence surrounding the field, and leave it enough slack so that it can graze half of the area of the field. Should the tether be equal to the radius of the field, shorter than the radius, or longer than the radius?

United Kingdom
1748AD

SEE ANSWER 92

 BUFFON'S NEEDLE

A truly astounding method for approximating pi was discovered by Georges-Louis Leclerc, Comte de Buffon, an 18th century French mathematician and naturalist. The technique derived from a question that Buffon posed in one of his books: if a floor is made up of parallel, equal-width strips of wood, what is the probability that a needle, dropped onto the floor, will cross one of the seams?

The solution to the problem turns out to be reasonably straightforward, albeit a bit tricky to get to. The probability P that the needle will cross a seam depends on the needle's length, L, and the distance between seams, d. Given these, the answer turns out to be $P = {}^{2L}/_{pi \cdot d}$. You can simplify this by making sure that the needle is the same length as the space between seams, in which case $P = {}^{2}/_{pi}$, and therefore $pi = {}^{2}/_{P}$, which broken down, means pi = 2 * (the number of total throws) / (the number of throws where the needle crosses a seam). In other words, amazingly, you can work out pi just by tossing a lot of needles onto a floor and counting how many cross seams.

But why?

France
1777AD

SEE ANSWER 93

The Thunderer

This traditional riddle is thought to have originated on the American frontier in the late 18th century.

I have a cock who needs no grain,
I keep him as a wonder.
Every time my cock does crow,
It lightens, hails and thunders.

United States
of America
c. 1800AD

SEE ANSWER 94

THE MINER

This is a riddle from 19th century America:

> I am snatched roughly from my home underground,
> Locked in a prison of cruel wood.
> I will never be released, yet
> I remain useful to all of you, and so
> I may be found in all manner of places.
> Who am I?

United States of America
c. 1820AD

SEE ANSWER 95

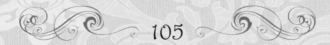

THE BLIND ABBOT

The Victorian era saw the development of large middle classes – with middle class obsessions – on both sides of the Atlantic. Puzzles and prurience were both in high fashion, as this puzzle shows.

In a convent, there were 24 monks of dubious piety and virtue, and an old, blind abbot. The convent had 9 chambers, laid out in a square. The abbot stayed in the centre, and the monks were chambered in groups of three in the remaining eight chambers. At night, the abbot would make rounds of the cells, counting the inhabitants. Provided he found nine monks in each line of three cells, he was satisfied that all was well.

The monks, taking advantage of his mathematical naivety, quickly discovered how to not only arrange themselves so that six of their number could sneak out to the nearby town, but even contrived to smuggle in a dozen ladies of dubious reputation. The abbot, finding his count at nine heads per row each time, was none the wiser.

How did they do it?

United States of America
c. 1850AD

SEE ANSWER 96

The Captive Queen

Lewis Carroll had a great fondness for puzzles and riddles of all sorts, from the most physically rooted through to the mathematically abstract. The puzzle of the Captive Queen harks back somewhat to the early puzzles of Alcuin of York, but provides its own fiendishly Carrollesque twist.

A queen and her children, one son and one daughter, are held captive in the top of a very tall tower. There is a pulley outside the window, over which runs a rope attached to an identical large basket at either end. When one basket is resting on the ledge outside the window, the other is on the ground. The queen weights 195lbs, her daughter 105lbs, her young son 90lbs, and they have a stone in the room, which weighs 75 pounds. The heavier basket will naturally sink to the ground, but if the weight discrepancy between the two baskets is greater than 15lbs, the descent will prove fatal to any living occupant.

How can the queen and her children escape?

United Kingdom
c. 1850AD

SEE ANSWER 97

SPIRAL WALK

This is one of Lewis Carroll's puzzles, and poses a seemingly simple mathematical question.

Picture an oblong garden, half a yard longer than it is wide. The entire surface of the garden is taken up with a gravel pathway, arranged in a rectangular spiral. The path is 1 yard wide, and 3,630 yards long. How wide is the garden?

United Kingdom
c. 1850AD

SEE ANSWER 98

EIGHT QUEENS

In 1848, German chess puzzle master Max Bezzel posed a tricky question whose ramifications have been engrossing mathematicians and puzzle experts ever since.

The challenge is to place eight queens on a regular 8x8 chess board so that none of them can attack any of the others – in other words, so that there is no vertical, horizontal or diagonal line that holds more than one queen.

Can you do it?

Germany
1848AD

SEE ANSWER 99

The Dinner Party

One of Lewis Carroll's better known and more convoluted puzzles involves the small imaginary nation of Kgovjni. One evening, the Governor of Kgovjni decides to throw a very small dinner party. To this end, he invites his father's brother-in-law, his brother's father-in-law, his father-in-law's brother, and his brother-in-law's father.

How many guests are there?

United Kingdom
c. 1850AD

SEE ANSWER 100

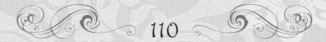

THE MONKEY AND THE PULLEY

Lewis Carroll devised this puzzle to illustrate the workings of momentum and force.

Imagine that there is a weightless, perfectly flexible rope strung over a frictionless pulley attached to a solid surface at a point higher off the floor than the rope is long. A monkey is hanging on to one end of the rope. A weight is hanging off the other end, horizontally level with the monkey, perfectly balancing it.

What happens when the monkey starts to climb towards the pulley – will the weight rise, fall or stay still?

United Kingdom
c. 1850AD

SEE ANSWER 101

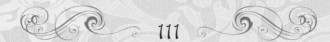

Kirkman's Schoolgirls

Thomas Kirkman was an English mathematician during the Victorian era who made a number of important contributions in the field of group theory. In *The Lady's and Gentleman's Diary* in 1850, he posed his Schoolgirl problem, for which he is best-known nowadays.

Fifteen young women are attending a school. They go for a daily walk in groups of three. Can they be arranged so that over the course of seven days, they never walk with the same person twice, and if so, can you work out how?

United Kingdom
1850AD

SEE ANSWER 102

The Counterfeit Bill

The Counterfeit Bill puzzle first appeared in William Henry Cremer's *The Magician's Own Book*, a handbook of conjuring and sleight of hand published in 1857.

A man goes into a hat shop to buy a top hat, presumably to produce his white rabbit from. The hat costs $6.30, and the man pays with a $10 bill. Some time after his departure, the hatter discovers to his dismay that the bill is a fake. How much money has he lost?

United States of America
1857 AD

SEE ANSWER 103

THE TRAVELLING SALESMAN

William Hamilton invented a puzzle called Around The World in 1859 which required the player to visit every node on a grid once and once only – in contrast to a Euler walk, in which the task is to visit every edge once and once only. Hamilton's first version was rather simplistic, but the idea has gone on to attract a lot of attention in the years since. This type of problem is now often known as a Travelling Salesman problem, from the idea that a salesman would not want to visit a town twice in close succession.

Is it possible to find a route on this graph that lets you visit each node once and once only, missing out one or more lines if you wish?

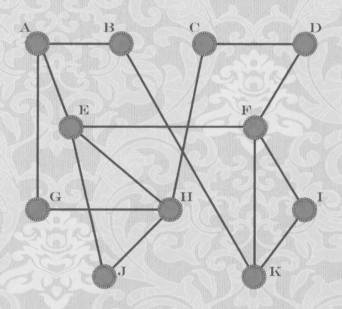

United States of America
1859 AD

SEE ANSWER 104

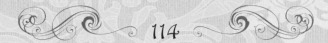 ETHIOPIAN MATHEMATICS

Although modern mathematical technique seems so natural to us as to be obvious, its familiarity is the result of our upbringing, and the problem of dealing with numbers has been solved repeatedly in history. A recollection from the turn of the 19th century graphically illustrated an approach used in ancient Ethiopia, as well as a range of different places around the world.

An army colonel was accompanying a local headman on a trip which included buying some cattle. The headman wanted to purchase 7 bulls, at a cost of $22 each. Lacking a formalised system of decimal multiplication, the headman and the herder sent for a local priest to calculate the total price.

The priest had his assistant dig two parallel columns of holes. In the first column, he put seven stones, for the number of bulls, in the first hole, and then doubled the number of stones for each subsequent hole
– 14, 28, 56 and 112. In the second column, he put 22 stones for the price of one bull in the first hole, and then halved the number of stones for each subsequent hole, rounding down – 11, 5, 2 and 1.

Considering even values to be evil, the priest went down the second column, and any time he found an even number of stones -- 22 and 2, in this instance -- he removed the stones from that hole, and from the first column hole next to it (7 and 56 respectively). Then he added the remaining stones in the first column, which came to 154, which is indeed 22 * 7.

This method will always work. But why?

Ethiopia
c. 1875AD

SEE ANSWER 105

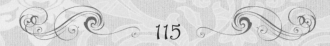

Cantor's Infinities

Georg Cantor was a German mathematician, born in 1845. He created set theory, which has become one of the fundamental theoretical underpinnings of modern mathematics. Logical exploration of set theory quickly took him into explorations of infinity, and during his 30s, he published a series of ground-breaking proofs regarding infinite sets. Many of them do not make intuitive sense.

Consider the set of all natural numbers, 0, 1, 2, 3, 4, ... and so on. The set is trivially provable as infinite – assume a maximum number X, then add 1 to it, and it is no longer the maximum. Now consider the set of all even numbers, 2, 4, 6, 8, ... This is provably infinite, too.

Which is larger?

Germany
1878 AD

SEE ANSWER 106

OBODY

This Victorian riddle remains relevant today:

I never was, am always to be,
No-one has ever or will yet meet me,
But I am the confidence of all
Who live and breathe on our spinning ball.
Who am I?

United Kingdom
c. 1880AD

SEE ANSWER 107

TESSERACT

The tesseract was first conceived of in 1888 by the mathematician and sci-fi writer Charles Howard Hinton. Hinton had a strong interest in multi-dimensional thinking, and even coined the now-common terms 'ana' and 'kata' for movement into and out of the fourth dimension, parallel to left and right, up and down, and forward and backward.

A tesseract is a four-dimensional hypercube, a cube which has a cube on each of its faces. That's obviously impossible to visualise accurately as a human, but the diagram shown here is a two-dimensional representation of it. Look at it for a while, and you'll spot a group of cubes in perspective view, jumbled together in there.

When you number the vertexes of this particular depiction of a tesseract as shown, you can then use the resulting pattern to very quickly generate a number of pandiagonal 4-order magic squares.

How?

United Kingdom
1888AD

SEE ANSWER 108

 ERTRAND'S BOX

In his 1889 work on probability, French mathematician Joseph Bertrand devised this interesting problem that has come to be known as Bertrand's Box.

Imagine that there are three boxes. One box contains two gold coins, one contains two silver coins, and one contains one gold and one silver. The boxes are mixed up, and you draw a coin at random from one of them. The coin you receive is gold. What is the chance that the other coin in the same box is also gold?

France
1889 AD

SEE ANSWER 109

OTHING LOST

This paradoxical brain-teaser was often inflicted on Victorian school children.
Forty-five can be subtracted from forty-five in such as way as to leave forty-five as a remainder. But how?

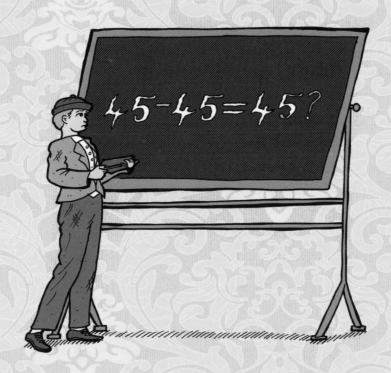

United Kingdom
c. 1890AD

SEE ANSWER 110

HILBERT'S HOTEL

David Hilbert was born in Königsberg in Germany – the city of the famous Seven Bridges problem (*see* page 99) – in 1862. He became one of the most important mathematicians of the early 20th century, and made a number of fundamental discoveries and methodological breakthroughs.

In the Paradox of the Grand Hotel, Hilbert suggested a theoretical hotel with an infinite number of rooms, each of them occupied. Suddenly, an infinite number of guests turn up, demanding to be accommodated. The proprietor of the hotel (some have suggested that he ought to be VALIS, after Philip K. Dick's infinite being) announces that he can indeed do so.

But how?

Germany
1895AD

SEE ANSWER 111

WINE/WATER PROBLEM

This puzzle, formalised by the Victorian mathematician W. W. R. Ball in his book *Mathematic Recreations*, was one of Lewis Carroll's favourites.

Imagine that you have two barrels holding equal volumes of wine and water. A cup of wine is taken and poured into the water, and mixed thoroughly. Then an identical cup of the wine/water mix is poured back into the wine, restoring both barrels to their previous volume, and again mixed thoroughly.

Which of the mixtures will be the purer?

United Kingdom
1896AD

SEE ANSWER 112

THE BARBER PARADOX

Betrand Russell was an extremely influential British philosopher, mathematician and social reformer. A fierce humanitarian and anti-war campaigner, he won the Nobel Prize in Literature in 1950, at the age of 78, for his philosophical and humanist work. As a philosopher, Russell believed in the application of logic to thought, and the utility of common sense and plain language in philosophical discourse. Suppose that there is a village with just one barber, a man. All the men of the village are required to be clean-shaven. Some shave themselves; the others are required to make use of the barber, who is obligated to shave only all those men who do not shave themselves.

Who shaves the barber?

United Kingdom
c. 1900AD

SEE ANSWER 113

Mamma's Age

Henry Dudeney, 1857–1930, was one of Britain's greatest puzzle geniuses. A mathematician, amateur theologian, self-taught shepherd and civil servant, he had a broad knowledge base and a love of playing with numbers. He was also a keen student of chess, particularly in his early years. His wife, Alice, was a celebrated author herself, and was frequently compared to Thomas Hardy for her dramatic and realistically-framed tales of rural life.

Dudeney wrote puzzles throughout his life, most of which continue to have a strong influence on puzzling in the modern era. His puzzles were marked by a certain gentleness, which comes through clearly in this puzzle.

Tommy: "How old are you, mamma?"

Mamma: "Let me think, Tommy. Well, our three ages add up to exactly 70 years."

Tommy: "That's a lot, isn't it? And how old are you, papa?"

Papa: "Just six times as old as you, my son."

Tommy: "Shall I ever be half as old as you, papa?"

Papa: "Yes, Tommy; and when that happens our three ages will add up to exactly twice as much as today."

Tommy: "And supposing I was born before you, papa; and supposing mamma had forgot all about it, and hadn't been at home when I came; and supposing–"

Mamma: "Supposing, Tommy, we talk about bed. Come along, darling. You'll have a headache."

Now, if Tommy had been some years older he might have calculated the exact ages of his parents from the information they had given him. Can you find out the exact age of mamma?

United Kingdom
c. 1900 AD

SEE ANSWER 114

Papa's Problem

Dudeney based this problem on a puzzle set by the last of the great Greek philosopher-mathematicians, Pappus, a teacher in Alexandria during the 4th century. Even as the sciences were crumbling into the dark ages, Pappus' work retained marvellous sophistication. Dudeney called his formulation Papa's Problem as an extra challenge, to see who would get the reference.

The little girl's Papa has taken two differently-sized pieces of cardboard, suspended them from threads, and clipped a piece from one so that it hangs level, as shown in the illustration. His daughter's task is to find the place on the unclipped card that will produce the same result without any trial and error.

Can you deduce a suitable spot?

United Kingdom
c. 1900AD

SEE ANSWER 115

KITE PROBLEM

Henry Dudeney contrived this interesting puzzle based around an apocryphal trip to a kite-flying competition on the Sussex Downs in England.

Professor Highflite was flying a kite attached to a perfectly tight spherical ball of wire. The ball was two feet in diameter, while the wire had a diameter of one hundredth of an inch. To within the nearest mile, how long was the wire?

Readers unused to converting inches to miles may prefer to calculate the length of the wire in inches, to the nearest ten thousand.

United Kingdom
c. 1900AD

SEE ANSWER 116

THE BARREL OF BEER

A vintner purchased a number of sealed barrels of drink, seven containing wine and one containing beer, as seen here. He kept the beer for himself, and then sold the wine to two people, one of whom purchased twice as much wine by volume as the other did.

Which barrel contains the beer?

United Kingdom
c. 1900AD

SEE ANSWER 117

THE CENTURY PUZZLE

Henry Dudeney composed this puzzle in honour of Édouard Lucas, the French mathematician, noting that Lucas had found seven different ways of writing 100 as a mixed natural + fractional number in which each of the digits from 1 to 9 was used just once. For example, $91 + 5^{742}/_{638}$ is one method. There is just one way of doing it, however, that has its natural component taking up just 1 digit (ie being less than 10).

Can you find it?

United Kingdom
c. 1900 AD

SEE ANSWER 118

THE LABOURER'S PUZZLE

In this puzzle, Dudeney challenges you to think both logically and precisely.

Professor Rackbrane, during one of his rambles, chanced to come upon a man digging a deep hole.

"Good morning," he said. "How deep is that hole?"

"Guess," replied the labourer. "My height is exactly five feet ten inches."

"How much deeper are you going?" said the professor.

"I am going twice as deep," was the answer, "and then my head will be twice as far below ground as it is now above ground."

Rackbrane now asks if you could tell how deep that hole would be when finished.

United Kingdom
c. 1900AD

SEE ANSWER 119

FENCE PROBLEM

Imagine that there is a perfectly square field, out in the Iowa countryside. The owner wishes to fence it in using a wooden fence made up of 2.75 yard bars, with seven bars in each section of fence. What's more, he wants to ensure that the fence contains exactly as many bars as the field has acres. It will help you to know that 1 acre is 4,840 square yards.

What is the size of the field?

United Kingdom
c. 1900AD

SEE ANSWER 120

Pierrot's Puzzle

This puzzle makes use of the interesting self-referential quality of some multiplications. The sum 15 * 93, as shown in the image, yields an answer made of exactly the same digits, just rearranged – 1395. If you try this with a total of three different digits on the two sides, there are just two possibilities, 3 * 51 = 153 and 6 * 21 = 126.

Assuming that you can split your digits 2x2 or 1x3 across the multiplication, can you find all the (few) ways that four different digits can be multiplied to yield an answer which contains only the same digits? It may help you to know that all of the possible results are less than 4000.

United Kingdom
c.1900AD

SEE ANSWER 121

THE FOUR SEVENS

$$(5+5) \times (5 \times 5) = 100$$

As Dudeney shows in the illustration here, it is easy to use four 5s to create a sum that equals 100. He then points out that four 9s would also be fairly easy to do, in the form of 99 + $^9/_9$. Achieving it with just four 7s is somewhat trickier.

Can you manage it?

United Kingdom
c. 1900AD

SEE ANSWER 122

Mr Gubbins in the Fog

London's notorious smog used to make it almost impossible to tell night from day. On one such occasion, Mr. Gubbins found himself forced to work by candle-light, because the fog came with a power cut. He had two candles, one of which he knew to last for four hours, and the other to last for five hours.

When he finished working, Mr. Gubbins discovered that one of the candle stubs was exactly four times the length of the other one.

How long was he working by candle-light?

United Kingdom
c. 1900AD

SEE ANSWER 123

THE BASKET OF POTATOES

In this Dudeney puzzle, a man had a basket of 50 potatoes. As a game, he laid the potatoes out on the ground in a straight line. The distance between the first two potatoes was one yard, increasing by two yards for each subsequent potato, so 3 yards to potato 3, 5 yards to 4, and so on. He then placed a basket by the first potato, and challenged his son to pick them all up and put them back in the basket, carrying only one at a time.

How far would his poor son have to travel to collect all the potatoes?

United Kingdom
c. 1900AD

SEE ANSWER 124

HE LOCKERS

This fiendish little Dudeney puzzle tells the tale of a whimsical clerk who was told to number three different 3x3 locker cupboards with single digits, and to make sure that no digit was repeated on any one cupboard. The boss expected to get three lockers each numbered 1–9, but he forgot that 0 is a digit too, and that no explicit numbering scheme had been specified.

When he returned, he found that his clerk had arranged the numbers so that for each cupboard A, B and C, the sum of the top two rows of digits gave the bottom row, and the 0 did not appear in the hundreds spot in any of the nine rows, so that each one was a regular three-digit whole number. Furthermore, the bottom row of A contained the lowest possible such sum, the bottom row of C contained the highest possible sum, and B was chosen so that no digit was repeated across the bottom rows of A, B and C.

How had the eccentric clerk numbered the lockers?

United Kingdom
c. 1900AD

SEE ANSWER 125

ODD MULTIPLICATION

Henry Dudeney had a fascination with puzzles and numbers that made use of interesting selections and patterns of digits. In this problem, he says, "If I multiply 51,249,876 by 3 (thus using all the nine digits once, and once only), I get 153,749,628 (which again contains all the nine digits once). Similarly, if I multiply 16,583,742 by 9 the result is 149,253,678, where in each case all the nine digits are used. Now, take 6 as your multiplier and try to arrange the remaining eight digits so as to produce by multiplication a number containing all nine once, and once only. You will find it far from easy, but it can be done."

United Kingdom
c. 1900 AD

SEE ANSWER 126

CURIOUS NUMBERS

Dudeney takes great pleasure in pointing out that 48 has an interesting peculiarity. If you add 1 to it, the result (49) is square. But if you halve it and add one, the result (25) is also square. There are of course infinitely many whole numbers that share this trait, although 48 is the first.

But can you find the next largest? How about the two after that?

United Kingdom
c. 1900AD

SEE ANSWER 127

CHANGING PLACES

This is one of Dudeney's more interesting time-related puzzles. The clock-face illustrated here shows a time slightly before 4:42. The hands will get back to exactly the same spots shortly after 8:23, so you could say that the hands will have changed places. Remember that we are talking about a clock whose hands constantly sweep smoothly, so the time of the minute hand fixes the relative location of the hour hand between hours. Taking this into account, how many times will the hands of a clock change places between 3pm and midnight? And considering all of the pairs of times indicated by these changes, what is the exact time when the minute hand will be nearest to the 45-minute mark?

United Kingdom
c. 1900AD

SEE ANSWER 128

The nine counters

In this Dudeney puzzle, the digits 1–9 are arranged as shown, as two multiplication sums, one a 3-digit number multiplied by a 2-digit number, the other two 2-digit numbers multiplied together. You can easily verify that 158 * 23 = 79 * 46 = 3634.

Rearranging the digits but keeping the same distribution pattern of numbers, and not duplicating any digit, what is the largest common result of the two multiplication sums that you can find?

United Kingdom
c. 1900AD

SEE ANSWER 129

DONKEY RIDING

Taking donkey-rides at the seaside is a long-standing British holiday tradition – perhaps because the sometimes-chilly British waters can be a little inhospitable.

In this puzzle, a pair of children try to have a donkey race. Whilst the donkeys are happy enough to trot along, they're friendly enough to each other to go at the same speed, no matter what their riders might prefer, and the race ends, naturally enough, in a dead heat.

However, the volunteer judges observe that the first half was run in the same time as the last half, the third quarter was run in the same time as the final quarter, and the first three quarters took six and three quarter minutes.

How long did the race take?

United Kingdom
c. 1900AD

SEE ANSWER 130

THE SPOT ON THE TABLE

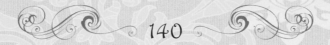

In this Dudeney puzzle, a young boy challenges his father to work out the diameter of a table jammed into the corner of a room. The table's edge has a spot on it on the side closest to the corner, and boy points out that the spot is eight inches from one wall and nine inches from the other.

What is the diameter of the table?

United Kingdom
c. 1900AD

SEE ANSWER 131

Catching the Thief

In this Dudeney puzzle, a policeman is chasing after a crook. The thief has a twenty-seven step head-start over the constable, and takes eight steps to the constable's five. However, the constable's stride is much longer, and two of his steps equal five of the thief's.

How many steps does it take for the policeman to catch the thief?

United Kingdom
c. 1900AD

SEE ANSWER 132

WHAT WAS THE TIME?

This Dudeney puzzle provides a fun challenge. If you add one quarter of the time from noon until now to half the time from now until noon tomorrow, you will get the time exactly.

What is the time?

United Kingdom
c. 1900AD

SEE ANSWER 133

THE THIRTY-THREE PEARLS

Dudeney's Thirty-Three Pearls problem is comparatively straightforward. There is a string of 33 pearls worth a massive £65,000. The pearls are arranged so that the biggest and most expensive is in the central spot. The individual pearls start out cheapest on each end. From one end, they increase by a uniform £100 up to and including the big pearl; from the other end, they increase by £150 up to and including the big pearl.

What is the value of the big pearl?

United Kingdom
c. 1900AD

SEE ANSWER 134

THE THREE VILLAGES

In the Three Village puzzle, Dudeney offers a somewhat obfuscated trigonometric challenge.

You set out to drive from Acrefield to Butterford, but accidentally find yourself going via the Cheesebury route, which is nearer to Acrefield than to Butterford, and is 12 miles precisely left of the direct road. When you then arrive at Butterford, you discover that you have travelled 35 miles. Each of the three roads is straight, and a whole number of miles in length.

What are the distances between the three villages?

United Kingdom
c. 1900AD

SEE ANSWER 135

ETERNAL

This Victorian riddle remains popular in the modern day:

> I am the beginning of eternity,
> I am the end of time and space,
> I am the start of every end,
> I am the end of every place.
> Who am I?

United Kingdom
c.1900D

SEE ANSWER 136

THE VILLAGE SIMPLETON

In puzzles, as in real life, it is never wise to patronisingly underestimate people with a seeming lack of formal education. In this puzzle, Dudeney tells of a somewhat supercilious city gent in the country who, wanting directions but not trusting the intelligence of the man he has found sitting on a stile, asks him the foolish question of which day it is. The baffling reply is that when the day after tomorrow is yesterday, today will be as far from Sunday as today was from Sunday when the day before yesterday was tomorrow.

Can you say what day it is?

United Kingdom
c. 1900AD

SEE ANSWER 137

WHAPSHAW'S WHARF MYSTERY

The Whapshaw's Wharf Mystery uses the framing device of a violent robbery and a murdered night watchman. The poor watchman was dumped in the river after being killed, and the water immediately caused his pocket watch to stop working. That would have given the time of the robbery, had one foolish policeman not tried to get the watch working again, and scrambled the time. When asked about it later, all the hapless constable could recall was that the second-hand had just passed 49, and that the hour and minute hand were perfectly aligned together.

If you know that the hands on the watch were of the constantly sweeping variety, rather than the type which clicks from division to division, what was the time on the watch when it stopped?

United Kingdom
c. 1900AD

SEE ANSWER 138

THE SPIDER AND THE FLY

A spider wants to make his way across a room to get to a fly. The room's end walls are 12 foot square, and its length is 30 feet. The spider is one foot below the ceiling in the centre of one end wall, whilst the fly is one foot above the ground in the centre of the other end wall.

Obeying the laws of gravity, what is the shortest distance that the spider has to travel to get to the fly's position? This is one of Henry Dudeney's more famous puzzles.

United Kingdom
1903AD

SEE ANSWER 139

CIRCLING THE SQUARES

This is a fiendish little Dudeney puzzle. In the circle, any two adjacent numbers, squared and then added together, should be equal to their diametrically opposite two numbers squared and added. No number needs to be bigger than 100, there should be no fractions, and no numbers are repeated.

Can you fill in the remaining six numbers?

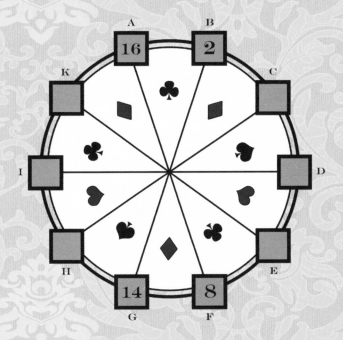

United Kingdom
c. 1905AD

SEE ANSWER 140

 CHARLEY AND MISS LOFTY

Sam Loyd was born in 1841, and grew up in New York city. He was an avid chess-player, and became one of the best players in the USA, rising to 15th in the world. He could almost certainly have done even better, but he had a propensity to attempt to create the most intricate situations on the board rather than simply going for the throat. He was also America's most important puzzle author of the late 1800s and early 1900s, doing a lot to define the general style of puzzles and riddles for decades to come. Even today, with our modern interest in abstract puzzles like Sudoku, his influence remains strong, and the following pages will have a selection of some of his best work. We'll open with a simple little riddle to give the flavour of Loyd's work.

Charley Lightop was attempting to woo the somewhat distant Miss Alice Lofty. "I say, Alice, I just thought of an original conundrum," said Charley. "Why is the moon like a suit of clothes?"

How do you imagine Miss Lofty replied?

United States of America
c. 1905AD

SEE ANSWER 141

CAST ASHORE

There has always been something romantic about the notion of the message in a bottle. In this puzzle, Loyd gives a cryptic little note from a washed-up bottle:

A mighty ship I now command,
With passengers from every land.
No goods have I to trade or sell,
Each wind will serve my turn as well.
I'm neither port nor harbour bound,
My greatest wish to run aground.

The note contains within it everything required to identify the hallowed author. Who is it?

United States of America
c. 1905AD

SEE ANSWER 142

THE BANK OF MONTE CARLO

In this probability-theory puzzle, Loyd posits a side-show gambling game involving the throw of dice.

In the game, a board is divided into six numbered squares, and gamblers are invited to place a stake on whichever number/s they choose. Three regular dice are then thrown, and whoever has correctly placed a stake on a number that comes up gets their stake back, plus the same again for each time their number has come up. So someone betting $1 on 2 when 2, 2, 5 was thrown would get $1 + 2 * $1 (i.e. $3) back.

What is the chance of winning?

United States of America
c. 1905AD

SEE ANSWER 143

THE ST PATRICK'S DAY PARADE

St Patrick's Day, March 17, has often been the occasion for festive parades, and in larger American cities such as New York, these often get very big indeed.

In this Loyd puzzle, a parade group finds itself one person short. They form up in rows of 10, but find that they have one space in the last row. They know that 11 will not work, so try rows of 9, 8, 7, etc, all the way down to 2. There is always one space in the last row. Eventually, the leader gives up and settles with single file.

How many marchers are there at a minimum?

United States of America
c. 1905 AD

SEE ANSWER 144

THE BOARDING HOUSE PIE

The Mystery of the Boarding House Pie is an interesting geometric challenge. The boarding house landlady has a circular pie with which she intends to feed her guests. She divides the pie with six straight lines, each of which intersects all five of the other lines. Each intersection however consists of just two lines touching, and leaves the landlady with a selection of sizes and shapes of pie to play favourites to her heart's content.

How is the pie to be divided?

United States of America
c. 1905AD

SEE ANSWER 145

DOMESTIC COMPLICATIONS

Loyd's Domestic Complications puzzle is an interesting hark-back to some of Lewis Carroll's constructions.

Smith, Jones and Brown were great friends, and after Brown's wife died, his niece helped him around the home. Smith was also a widower, and lived with his daughter. When Jones got married, his wife, thinking of the two other men and the generous size of her own home, suggested that they all come and live together.

To ensure equitability, each member of the household, male and female, was to contribute $25 a month towards household expenses. Whatever remained at the end of the month would be distributed equally. The first month's expenses were $92.00. When the remainder was distributed, each received an even number of dollars, without fractions or anything left over. How much did each receive, and why?

United States of America
c. 1905AD

SEE ANSWER 146

THE CONVENT

Loyd draws upon the earlier puzzle of the Blind Abbot in this question, which is somewhat more complex than its older forebear.

Centuries ago, the convent of Mt. Maladetta in the Pyrenees was a square three-story building with eight rooms on each of the top two floors, arranged around a central courtyard. These top floors provided sleeping accommodation, with twice as many nuns sleeping on the top floor as one the one below. The elderly mother superior arranged matters so that each room was occupied, and that on each side of the building, the two floors together housed 11 nuns.

After the French army retreated through the area, the nuns discovered that nine of their youngest and prettiest members had vanished, presumed stolen away by the soldiers. To avoid upsetting the mother superior, they rearranged themselves so that they still abided by all of the mother superior's conditions regarding sleeping arrangements. The mother superior was none the wiser.

How many nuns were there, and how were they arranged?

United States of America
c. 1905AD

SEE ANSWER 147

 LD BEACON TOWER

In this puzzle, Loyd describes an apocryphal ruined tower on the Jersey coast. When originally built, the tower was 300 feet high, and surrounded by a staircase which circled the tower exactly four times from bottom to top. The steps were enclosed by a banister, which had one support every step. Given that each support was one foot from the next, and the tower was 23 feet 10½ inches in diameter (staircase included), how many steps were there?

United States of America
c. 1905AD

SEE ANSWER 148

CASEY'S COW

Rail bridges don't usually leave pedestrian space either side of the track. Why would they? In this puzzle, Loyd tells us that Casey's cow was standing on a single-track rail bridge when she spotted a train approaching at 90mph, just two bridge-lengths away from entering the bridge. Rather than run away from the train – which would have left her with her rearmost 3 inches caught on the bridge – she ran towards the train, and made it off the bridge with a foot to spare.

If the cow was standing 5 feet from the middle of the bridge, how long is the bridge?

United States of America
c. 1905AD

SEE ANSWER 149

HOT CROSS BUNS

Drawing on Mother Goose's nursery rhymes – quite contemporary at the time – Loyd constructed this puzzle, based on the extended cry of the hot cross bun vendor.

"Hot cross buns, hot cross buns, one-a-penny, two-a-penny, hot cross buns.
  If your daughters don't like 'em, give 'em to your sons!
  Two-a-penny, three-a-penny, hot cross buns.
  I had as many daughters as I had sons,
  So I gave them seven pennies to buy their hot cross buns."

Assuming that buns come in three sizes as described in the rhyme, and each child got the same number of (intact) buns, how many children are there and how many buns did each receive?

United States of America
c. 1905AD

SEE ANSWER 150

CYPHER DISPATCH PUZZLE

In cryptography, one of the most basic tools is knowing the relative frequency of occurrence of letters in the English language. These are: a, 83; b, 16; c, 30; d, 44; e, 120; f, 25; g, 17; h, 64; i, 80; j, 4; k, 8; l, 40; m, 30; n, 80; o, 80; p, 17; q, 5; r, 62; s, 80; t, 90; u, 34; v, 12; w, 20; x, 4; y, 20; z, 2.

The following cipher is a simple substitution, where each letter is consistently replaced by a different letter, and word structures remain as they were. Can you decipher the text and answer the puzzle it gives?

Ted skaage rj terj. Qdt kj jkssbjd teft Gefwqdj rj bid terwn wrgedw tefi Dqqdi. Tedi eba hkge sbbwdw rj Dqqdi tefi Gefwqdj?

United States of America
c. 1905AD

SEE ANSWER 151

THE FIGHTING FISHES OF SIAM

There are, according to Loyd, two types of fish found in Siam which despise each other – the large white perch, called the king fish, and the small black carp, called the devil fish. These species inevitably attack each other on sight. What the devil fish lack in size, they make up for in perfect strategy and in numbers. Three devil fish exactly counterbalance one king fish, to the point of stalemate, but four can kill a king fish in 3 minutes, with each additional fish making the new group proportionally quicker than the one before.

If there are four king fish and thirteen devil fish, which side would win, and how long would it take them to do so?

United States of America
c. 1905AD

SEE ANSWER 152

THE GOLF PUZZLE

The golf puzzle hypothesises a situation where a golfer wants to learn just two shots, one shorter and one longer, in order to master his nine-hole golf course. Assuming that the golfer will always be able to play directly to the hole, and will make a shot of the exact chosen distance each time, Loyd asks which two shot lengths should the golfer select to minimise the number of strokes required if the course's hole lengths are 150yds, 300yds, 250yds, 325yds, 275yds, 350yds, 225yds, 400yds and 425yds.

Can you find the solution?

United States of America
c. 1905AD

SEE ANSWER 153

PUZZLING SCALES

This puzzle is an early example of balancing scales using abstract quantities, a visual representation of simple algebra.

Given that the top two scales are in perfect balance, how many marbles are required to balance the bottom scale?

United States of America
c. 1905AD

SEE ANSWER 154

A LEGAL PROBLEM

In this puzzle, Loyd gives us a tricky little question of inheritance.

As a matter of legal importance, with fortunes at stake, the question is whether or not a man's marriage to his widow's sister can be considered legal or not.

United States of America
c. 1905AD

SEE ANSWER 155

THE NECKLACE

The Necklace puzzle was one of Loyd's subtler and more challenging puzzles, for all of the inherent simplicity of the question.

A lady goes into a jeweller's shop with 12 sections of chain identical to the ones bordering the diagram here. She wishes to have them fixed into one loop of chain of links, large and small. The jeweller explains that it costs 15 cents to cut and re-seal a small link, and 20 cents to cut and re-seal a big link.

What is the minimum cost of the completed chain?

United States of America
c. 1905AD

SEE ANSWER 156

THE BOXER PUZZLE

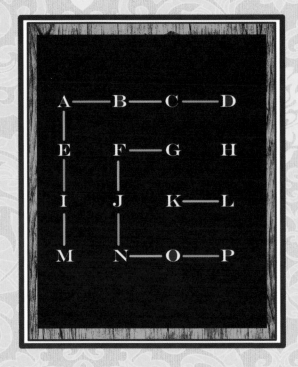

Loyd presents the game illustrated here as originating in China, although that is possibly a pun on 'boxes' and 'Boxer'. The playing field is a square grid of dots, and players take turns to connect two points with a single line. A player who completes a full box claims it for their own and must then immediately take another turn, so it is possible to get some quite long cascades.

   In this puzzle variant, the points are replaced by the letters A – P. Player 1 is due to take the next turn. What should player 1's next move be, and what will the result be assuming player 2 plays ideally?

United States of America
c. 1905AD

SEE ANSWER 157

THE PATROLMAN'S PUZZLE

In this Loyd puzzle, a policeman wants to maximize the number of houses he walks past on his beat. His orders state that he has to start his tour at the corner of 2nd and A, the spot on the edge of the houses directly below the top left corner. He has to walk an odd number of houses on each street and each avenue, returning to where he started.

His current route is illustrated below.

Can you find a route which takes in all the houses?

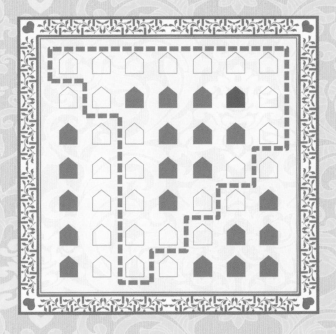

United States of America
c. 1905AD

SEE ANSWER 158

TURF PUZZLE

To show how little the patrons of the turf know about the theory of odds as practised at the race track, let readers seek a solution to the following elementary problem: If the odds are 7–3 against Apple Pie, 6–5 against Bumble Bee, and 83–27 against Cucumber, what first-past-the-post bet should a gambler make to be sure of not losing his money?

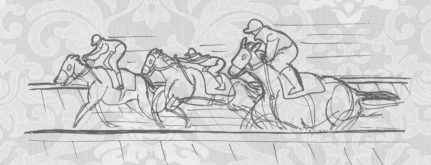

United States of America
c. 1905AD

SEE ANSWER 159

ASTRONOMICAL PUZZLE

This Loyd puzzle has a loosely astronomical theme. The grid is supposed to show the neighbourhood of a highly erratic comet. Starting from the small white star, make the shortest possible number of straight-line moves to run through the centre of each black star at least once and finish at the large white star.

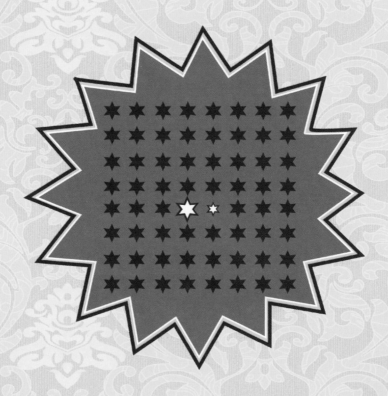

United States of America
c. 1905AD

SEE ANSWER 160

PATCH QUILT PUZZLE

Loyd's Patch Quilt Puzzle is an early ancestor of the modern word-search, perhaps even the first. The grid contains the names of a number of girls, reading from square to square, and each time moving in any direction, including diagonally. You can only use each square once per name, of course. You're given Nancy to start with – how many other girls are hidden in the square?

Primitive Railroading Problem

Loyd's Primitive Railroading problem is one of the classic puzzles in the field of motion and spatial arrangement.

Two trains are approaching each other along a stretch of one-way track, one with three carriages plus engine, and one with four carriages plus engine. There is a siding between them that is just large enough to hold a single carriage or engine. Carriages cannot be fastened to the front of an engine, nor can they be moved around by any means other than an engine.

How are the trains to pass each other?

United States of America
c. 1905AD

SEE ANSWER 162

THE ROGUE'S LETTER

An international gang of crooks have committed a great bank robbery in this Loyd puzzle. The gang are supposed to visit a series of 19 American cities, encoded in the following letter. Can you decipher them?

"Dear Jim – I won the race. The track was at the Olympic level and hard as cobalt. I more than won, for my position was central – eight before and eight behind. They had all a start from a half to a mile – to them a considerable advantage, but I can win on a run or walk and overtake and meander by – or kill – the best of them. Treading from early day to night the roads we follow.
ELLSWORTH."

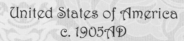

United States of America
c. 1905AD

SEE ANSWER 163

THE SQUAREST GAME

In this puzzle, Sam Loyd conjures up the sort of game you might find at a funfair. There are ten separate figures, each with its own point value. The aim is to knock over figures that will add up to a total of 50 points precisely, in order to win a small prize. You can have as many throws as you like – at a price, of course.

Which figures should you aim for?

United States of America
c. 1905

SEE ANSWER 164

SWARM OF GOOD BEES

A rebus is a visual word-play puzzle or pun. We have examples dating back to Ancient Egyptian hieroglyphic rebuses, and many heraldic designs are conceived as rebus word-plays, a technique which is known as canting. So Sam Loyd was tapping into a rich vein of historical thought when he derived this visual puzzle.

What are the useful New Year's resolutions depicted in the image?

WEARY WILLIE AND TIRED TIM

Train tracks were a much more hospitable walking route for 19th century vagrants than they are today, where high-speed trains, power lines and other hazards make them far too dangerous to approach. In this puzzle, Loyd introduces a pair of vagrants who meet each other coming and going.

Weary Willie is 10 miles from Joytown along the track to Pleasantville when he meets Tired Tim heading in the other direction. The two have been walking since dawn, so stop and chat for a while, and then continue on their way. They reach their destinations only to be immediately turned back the way they came. When they bump into each other again, they are 12 miles from Pleasantville.

How far is it from Joytown to Pleasantville?

United States of America
c. 1905AD

SEE ANSWER 166

BERRY'S PARADOX

In his 1927 work *Principia Mathematica*, the philosopher Bertrand Russell discussed a paradox which had been suggested to him some years before by G. G. Berry, a librarian at the Bodleian Library in Oxford. As Berry pointed out, there are only a finite number of words, and so only a finite – albeit large – number of possible phrases of 10 words or less, even allowing combinations that make no linguistic sense. This means that there are only so many ways to describe a number in less than 11 words. There are, however, an infinite number of numbers.

As Russell put it, that then means there must be a positive integer that is not definable in less than 11 words, and because integers are sequential, there must be a smallest positive integer that is not definable in under 11 words.

That integer, then, can be defined as "The smallest positive integer not definable in under 11 words" – a ten-word definition. So we are left with a paradox in which there has to be a smallest integer not definable in under 11 words, but that integer, in the fact of being that number, cannot actually be the smallest integer not definable in under 11 words.

Is there a resolution?

United Kingdom
c. 1910AD

SEE ANSWER 167

ROSSWORD

The mighty Crossword – the world's most successful puzzle to date – was created in 1913 by Arthur Wynne, a Liverpudlian journalist and puzzle creator. He invented the puzzle for the December 21 edition of the *New York World*, calling it Word-Cross. The puzzle rapidly became a sensation, and diversified into the various forms we are so familiar with today.

This is Arthur Wynne's historic first crossword.

2-3. What bargain hunters enjoy.
6-22. What we all should be.
4-5. A written acknowledgment.
4-26. A day dream.
6-7. Such and nothing more.
2-11. A talon.
10-11. A bird.
19-28. A pigeon.
14-15. Opposed to less.
F-7. Part of your head.
18-19. What this puzzle is.
22-23. An animal of prey.
26-27. The close of a day.
28-29. To elude.
10-18. The fibre of the gomuti palm.
8-9. To cultivate.
12-13. A bar of wood or iron.
16-17. What artists learn to do.
20-21. Fastened.
24-25. Found on the seashore.
30-31. The plural of is.

23-30. A river in Russia.
1-32. To govern.
33-34. An aromatic plant.
N-8. A fist.
24-31. To agree with.
3-12. Part of a ship.
20-29. One.
5-27. Exchanging.
9-25. Sunk in mud.
13-21. A boy.

United Kingdom
1913 AD

SEE ANSWER 168

THE HORSE PARADOX

The Horse Paradox was devised by Hungarian mathematician George Polya as an example of how mathematical and logical principles can be misapplied if you are not rigorous. Say there is a group of 5 horses. If you can prove that any group of 4 horses are the same colour, then, because you can break your set of 5 into subsets of 4 covering all possible combinations, the set of 5 has to be the same colour.

You can then use the same logical induction to say that you can prove groups of 4 are monochrome from sets of 3; groups of 3 from 2; and, finally, groups of 2 from 1. One horse is itself inevitably the same colour as itself, so all groups of horses are provably the same colour.

What's the flaw?

Austria
c.1922AD

SEE ANSWER 169

WASHING DAY

This American riddle has a rather domestic flavour:
What gets wet when drying?

United States of America
c. 1930AD

SEE ANSWER 170

ROPE AROUND THE EARTH

This is a fascinating puzzle, first introduced in the work of the English mathematician and philosopher William Whiston in 1702. This formulation comes from Germany in 1935.

The circumference of the Earth at the equator is 40,075.16 kilometres. Assuming for the sake of argument that the Earth were uniformly flat, imagine a rope tied around the equator and drawn tight, so that it is flush with the ground all the way around. If 10m of slack is added to the rope, and the rope raised uniformly until it is again taut and a uniform height above the Earth, how high off the ground would the rope be?

Germany
1935AD

SEE ANSWER 171

SCHRÖDINGER'S CAT

Erwin Schrödinger was one of the founders of quantum mechanics. A Nobel laureate and a close friend of Einstein's, Schrödinger devised a thought experiment which has become one of the most famous expressions of quantum mechanics.

A cat is penned up in a steel chamber, along with a device that will release a poisonous gas when a small bit of radioactive material decays – a process which is as close to truly random as we can find. There is a 50% chance that in any given hour, the material will decay, and the cat will be poisoned.

After an hour, what state is the cat in?

Austria
1935AD

SEE ANSWER 172

HEMPEL'S RAVENS

Carl Gustav Hempel, who died in 1997, was one of the 20th century's most important philosophers of science. He created, with Oppenheim, the dominant method of scientific explanation throughout the 1950s and 1960s, known as the Deductive-Nomological model. He also crafted a fascinating paradox based on logical principle.

If we consider the statement that (a) all ravens are black to be true, then by implication, (b) everything that is not black is not a raven. To get some evidence to support (a), we can observe that my pet raven, Nevermore, is black. To support (b) – which in turn supports (a) – we can observe that this green (and not black) item is an apple, not a raven.

Therefore, seeing a green apple proves that all ravens are black.

Where's the flaw?

Germany
1945AD

SEE ANSWER 173

TWO TRAINS

It is said that when the renowned mathematical genius John von Neumann was asked this puzzle, he managed to answer it immediately, by working it out the long way round!

Two trains are on a track heading towards each other. They are 100km apart, and are both travelling at 50km/h. There is a fly just in front of one train, and it gets scared and buzzes away down the track at 75km/h. When it reaches the other train, it reverses its direction and heads back up the track. How many kilometres does the fly travel before the trains collide?

United States of America
c. 1945AD

SEE ANSWER 174

THE UNEXPECTED HANGING

A relatively modern philosophical paradox was posited by D. O'Connor in 1948. A judge tells a condemned prisoner that he will be hanged at midday one weekday during the following week, and guarantees that the execution will be a surprise – he will not know the day until the executioner comes for him.

The prisoner reasons that if he gets to Friday, the last day possible, then there can be no surprise when he is called for, and so the execution cannot be Friday. That makes Thursday the last day possible – but then, if he gets to Thursday, he can't be surprised, so he can't be hung on the Thursday either. In fact, by similar reasoning, none of the days are possible. The judge has given his guarantee, so the prisoner reasons he will not be hanged.

He is therefore surprised when the executioner turns up on Wednesday morning.

What is the flaw in the prisoner's logic?

United States of America
1948AD

SEE ANSWER 175

THE SULTAN'S DOWRY

American mathematician Merrill Flood introduced the fiancée problem during a lecture in 1949. Since then it has been presented in a number of forms, including the secretary problem, the fussy suitor problem and the sultan's dowry problem, the form it is presented in here.

A sultan had 100 daughters, and granted a lucky commoner a chance at marrying one of them. The sultan told the commoner that he would be introduced to the girls one at a time, in no particular order, and told that girl's dowry as he met her. He had to immediately either say yes or no, and either decision was final. However, he would only be allowed to marry her if he picked the daughter with the greatest dowry.

What is the commoner's best chance of finding the right daughter?

United States of America
1949AD

SEE ANSWER 176

FERMI'S PARADOX

Italian Enrico Fermi was a remarkable scientist, and one of the leading physicists of the 20th century. He contributed greatly in a number of important areas, including quantum theory and nuclear physics, and was often remarked upon for his gentle modesty. Unlike most physicists, he was a master of both theory and experimentation, and won a Nobel Prize for his work on radioactivity. He sadly died in his early 50s of cancer acquired in the course of his work, but considered that cost worthwhile.

During a lunch-break at the Los Alamos National Laboratory in New Mexico, Fermi and some colleagues – Teller, Konopinsky and York – got into a light discussion about extra-terrestrials. A few minutes later, Fermi suddenly asked "Where are they?" He did some basic estimates regarding life in the universe, and arrived at the conclusion that Earth should already have been visited many times by aliens throughout history and pre-history, and that they – or at least the evidence of their civilisations – should be clearly visible.

There are some 250 billion stars in our galaxy, and hundreds of billions times that many visible to us. With so many planets out there, there must be a large number of civilisations in our galaxy alone. The Sun is a reasonably young star, so there could very easily be civilizations billions of years old in our galaxy. Why haven't they colonized it? At least, why can't we see the evidence of their passage?

Skeptics and religious thinkers have both used Fermi's paradox as proof that there is no intelligent extraterrestrial life. Are they right to do so?

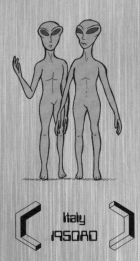

Italy
1950AD

SEE ANSWER 171

THE PRISONER'S DILEMMA

The Prisoner's Dilemma was created some time around 1950 by Melvin Dresher and Merrill Flood. It has become the *de facto* poster child for game theory.

Two criminals are arrested, separated and interviewed by the police. Each one is told that if he testifies against his comrade, then providing that the comrade does not implicate him, he can go free, while his comrade will get 10 years in prison. If each implicates the other, both will go down for 5 years each. If both remain silent, the police will only be able to jail the men for six months. No communication between the prisoners is possible, and the police guarantee not to let the other man know if he is betrayed. You can assume the two men are not close friends but bear no ill-will to each other, and would rather spend less time in prison than more.
How should the prisoners act?

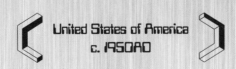

United States of America
c. 1950AD

SEE ANSWER 178

BOOK STACK

The book stacking problem has its roots in 19th century mathematical work, but wasn't properly formalised for almost a century.

   The challenge is to stack a set of identical, hard-back books on the edge of a desk so that they protrude over the edge as far as possible without falling down. You can get one book to balance at one-half length, and you can arrange four books to balance at one entire book's length. How many books do you think it will take to have the stack protrude for two books' length?

United States of America
1953AD

SEE ANSWER 179

Two Envelope Problem

The Two Envelope problem originated with Maurice Kraitchik, a Belgian mathematician, in 1953. He framed it somewhat differently, but the paradox has been consistent in form since Nalebuff's 1989 interpretation of it with a pair of envelopes as the objects of choice.

Imagine you are being offered two identical envelopes. Each contains a certain amount of cash, one twice the value of the other. You may select one envelope, and then you are given the option to swap the two, if you wish.

The problem lies in selection. Once you pick an envelope, the other can either contain half what you have, or twice what you have. The chance is 50–50. In risk management terms, the potential loss – 50% of your total, one time out of two – is 25%. The potential gain – 100% of your total, one time out of two – is 50%. So it is crazy not to swap. But once you swap, exactly the same logic applies, and you have to swap again, indefinitely, and you'll never select either envelope.

Where's the error?

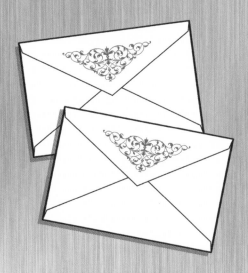

SEE ANSWER 180

POSTAGE STAMP PROBLEM

The postage stamp problem is a refinement of the number-theory work of German mathematician Ferdinand Frobenius, who died in 1917.

   Imagine there is a country whose postage stamp selection is limited to a reasonably small range. Given a maximum number of stamps that can fit on any one envelope, there must be a smallest postage price which the stamps cannot be used to make. Frobenius showed that the problem has no simple general resolution, so given the stamps 1, 4, 7 and 10, and an envelope which can only hold a maximum of four stamps, what is the lowest value of postage that you cannot make?

Germany
1955AD

SEE ANSWER 181

STABLE MARRIAGE PROBLEM

The Stable Marriage problem is an interesting way of looking at the dynamics of matching up two groups by preferential choice. Assume there are two groups of single people, one of men and one of women, of equal numbers, and that each person is able to produce an order of preference regarding marrying all the members of the opposite sex. The people are all going to pair off and marry. These marriages will be considered stable if there are no two people of the opposite sex who each prefer the other to their current partners.

American mathematicians David Gale and Lloyd Shapley devised an algorithm for pairing people that used a number of rounds to produce a solution. Each round, each unattached man proposes to the woman he likes the best out of the women he has not yet proposed to, whether she is attached or not. Afterwards, each woman provisionally agrees to engagement with the man she likes the best out of her still-unattached suitors. You can repeat the process until all the men (and therefore all the women) have partners.

Will the arrangement thus produced be stable?

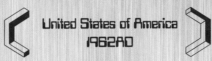

United States of America
1962AD

SEE ANSWER 182

Quine's Paradox

American philosopher and logician Willard Van Orman Quine spent almost all his adult life at Harvard University, going from student to Professor of Philosophy to retired emeritus. He espoused an Analytic doctrine, that the truth of a statement should be determined though the analysis of its meaning. Quine constructed his paradox as a modified form of the Cretan (Liar) Paradox.

This paradox is simple enough. It is the statement that:

"Yields falsehood when preceded by its quotation"
yields falsehood when preceded by its quotation.

If the statement is correct, it is invalidating itself by not giving falsehood, and therefore contradictory; if it is incorrect, it is verifying itself, which implies falsehood, and is therefore contradictory. Is there a way around it?

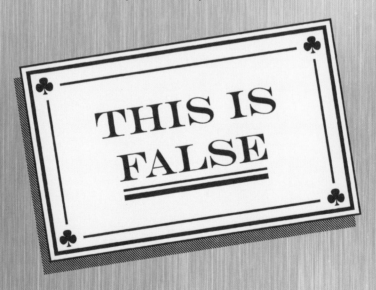

THIS IS
FALSE

 United States of America
1982AD

SEE ANSWER 183

Suiri

Logic-grid puzzles, known by a variety of names but increasingly, now, by the Japanese term Suiri, first made their appearance in the USA in 1962.

Five puzzle masters are spread across the British isles. Each one has a speciality which he is particularly adept at solving. From the information given below, can you say where each man lives, what his speciality is, and what his regular job is?

1. Bill lives in Essex. His speciality is neither Wordsearch nor Numberlink.
2. The Surrey man is a policeman. He is not the Crossword specialist, who is called Robert.
3. The driver lives in Norfolk.
4. The Suiri master is called Martin, and he is not a builder.
5. The tailor specialises in neither Sudoku nor Suiri, and he does not live in Yorkshire.
6. Ken does not live in Strathclyde.
7. The Wordsearch man is a farmer, and is not called John.

	SUIRI	SUDOKU	CROSSWORD	NUMBERLINK	WORDSEARCH	STRATHCLYDE	YORKSHIRE	NORFOLK	SURREY	ESSEX	FARMER	TAILOR	BUILDER	DRIVER	POLICEMAN
BILL															
ROBERT															
MARTIN															
KEN															
JOHN															
POLICEMAN															
DRIVER															
BUILDER															
TAILOR															
FARMER															
ESSEX															
SURREY															
NORFOLK															
YORKSHIRE															
STRATHCLYDE															

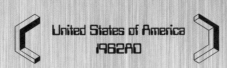

United States of America
1962AD

SEE ANSWER 184

THE BIRTHDAY PARADOX

It is an interesting quirk of probability that in a group of people, you are likely to find that there is a surprisingly high chance that two people share the same birthday. The probability calculations were discussed by McKinney in 1966, and it has become known as the Birthday Paradox because of its comparative counter-intuitiveness.

Assuming that the dates of birth are randomly spread, how many people do you need to have in a group for there to be at least a 50% chance that two share a birthday? How about to get a 99% chance?

United States of America
1966AD

SEE ANSWER 185

KAKURO

Kakuro started as an American puzzle, Cross-Sums, in *Dell Pencil Puzzles and Word Games*,1966. In 1980, a Japanese businessman called Maki Kaji was in Ireland for the 2,000 Guineas race. A dedicated puzzler, he found a Cross-Sums, and was instantly hooked. Back in Japan, he and a colleague started designing their own version, which they called Kakuro, from the Japanese for Add–Cross. The company they set up was named after the winner of that 2,000 Guineas – Nikoli. Since then, Nikoli have become one of the most powerful forces in the puzzle world, and their innovations are in every country. They popularised Sudoku, and Kakuro is their number two.

The rules are straightforward. Empty squares hold digits from 1 to 9 so that each unbroken line of numbers adds up to the clue value in the filled segment to its left (for horizontal lines) or above it (for vertical lines). No number may be used more than once in any unbroken line. Most people find a list of the different ways that each number can be made from two, three, four or even five digits helpful, bearing in mind that digits can't be repeated. Armed with this, and the knowledge that almost every square is part of at least two sums, all that remains is to apply some logic.

How is the grid filled?

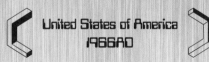

United States of America
1966AD

SEE ANSWER 188

WORDSEARCH

The first word-search puzzle that adheres exactly to the modern form was created by Norman Gilbat of Norman, Oklahoma, and published in the *Selenby Digest* of March 1, 1968. The *Digest,* a free wanted-ads paper distributed in the town's stores, came to the attention of teachers in the local schools. They spread it to colleagues, and eventually it came to the attention of puzzle syndicators, and then the world.

Words are hidden in the grid of letters in a straight line, and can be found orthogonally or diagonally, backwards or forwards. This one contains the names of 38 important figures from mathematics and puzzle history – all of whom you will find mentioned in this book.

Can you find them all?

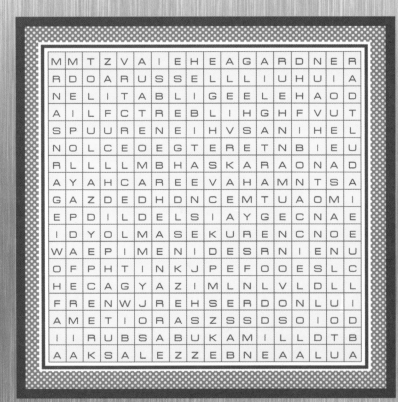

 United States of America
1968AD

SEE ANSWER 187

THE MONTY HALL PROBLEM

The Monty Hall problem was inspired by the American TV game show *Let's Make a Deal*, hosted most famously by Canadian presenter Monty Hall. The problem itself was first overtly posed by Steve Selvin in letters to *American Statistician*, drawing on earlier veridical paradoxes – particularly Martin Gardner's Three Prisoner Problem. A common formulation of the problem is as follows:

You are on a game show, and you have the choice of three doors. One hides a car, and the other two hide goats. You pick one, and Monty Hall, who knows what is behind the doors, opens one of the others, revealing a goat. He then offers you the chance to switch to the other unopened door. Is it to your advantage to switch?

SEE ANSWER 188

Meta Tic-Tac-Toe

Noughts and Crosses is a simplified form of a Roman game, *Terni Lapilli*, from around the time of Christ. The main differing feature of the earlier game is that each player had three counters, and once all six were in play, players then took turns to move one piece. In *Terni Lapilli*, a competent player opening with the centre square was guaranteed to win, although the popularity of the game for a while in ancient Rome suggests that this wasn't widely known.

By the time the game reached medieval Europe, the idea of moving pieces had gone, and Noughts and Crosses had taken its modern form. Competent players will always draw. If player one takes centre and his opponent does not take a corner, or if player one starts off-centre and his opponent does then not occupy the centre, it is possible for player one to force a victory. No other victories can be forced.

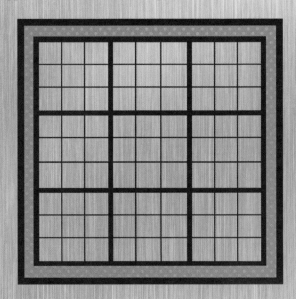

Meta Tic-Tac-Toe, described in 1978 by David Silverman in Volume 11 of the *Journal of Recreational Mathematics*, is a grid of Tic-Tac-Toe games themselves played on a 3x3 grid. The winner is the first person to win three smaller games that fall in a row on the larger grid. Player One opens with one move, after which all turns get two moves each, and moves can be marked anywhere on the larger grid. Assuming two competent players, if player one plays on the centre square of the centre board, who will win?

 United States of America 1978AD

SEE ANSWER 189

SUDOKU

Few people realize that the world-famous Sudoku was created by a retired Indiana puzzle enthusiast, Howard Garns. It is thought that Garns first devised his puzzle in the early 1960s, while working as an architect for Daggett. His puzzle, which he called 'Number Place', first appeared in 1979 in *Dell Pencil Puzzles and Word Games* magazine, becoming a reasonably regular feature of the magazine. Garns died in 1989, and although he never knew that he had created what would become the most phenomenally successful global puzzle since the crossword, he did live to see Sudoku become hugely popular in Japan in the mid-80s.

The rules of Sudoku are simple. Fill in the grid so that the numbers 1–9 appear exactly once in each row, column and 3x3 marked box. You don't need any mathematical skill, just some patient logical deduction. Most people start by pencil-marking each empty square with representations of all the numbers that could possibly be in that square, either writing the numbers themselves in them, or putting dots in a 3x3 grid in the space, so, for example, 1 is a dot top left, and 8 is a dot bottom centre. This method is more compact than writing numbers.

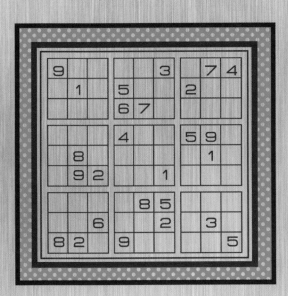

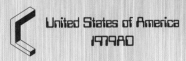

SEE ANSWER 190

NONOGRAM

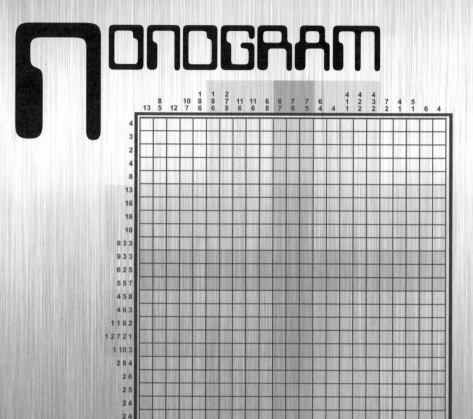

Nonograms first appeared in 1987 as a piece of conceptual art. Japanese graphic editor Non Ishida came up with the idea of using the windows of office blocks to create grid-based pictures, winning a Tokyo competition with the concept. Ishida then created three related puzzles, involving colouring squares in a grid according to logical principles. From there, Nonograms – the name was coined by English puzzler James Dalgety, who popularised the idea outside of Japan – rapidly became popular all over the world.

The rules are simple enough. A number of cells in the grid are to be shaded. Each row and column may contain one or more continuous lines of shaded cells, known as 'blocks'. The numbers adjacent to the row or column indicate the lengths of the different blocks contained in that line. Blocks are separated from other blocks in the same row or column by at least one empty cell. A picture will generally emerge when the cells are shaded correctly, although it is possible to solve the puzzle by logic alone, just from the intersections of the block numbers.

Where are the shaded cells?

Japan
1987AD

SEE ANSWER 191

SLITHERLINK

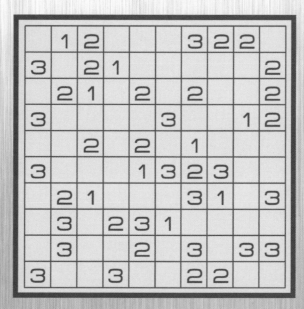

Nikoli's Slitherlink first appeared in 1989 as the fusion of two other puzzles. The game is played on the lines of a grid, with numbers in the grid cells showing how the lines are to be placed. A number of the grid lines have to be joined together to make one single complete loop. The numbers in the cell indicate how many of that cell's sides form part of the loop.

Where is the path?

Japan
1989AD

SEE ANSWER 192

202

HASHIWOKAKERO

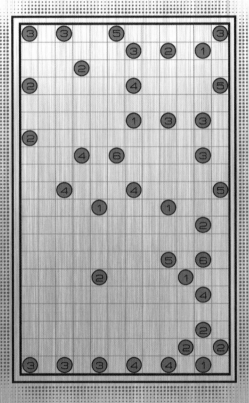

Hashi is another of Nikoli's world-beating contributions to puzzling. It is played on a grid-layout, and features a number of islands, each bearing a number. The islands are connected into one single group by a number of bridges, straight lines which run either horizontally or vertically between islands. The number on each island is the number of bridges connecting to it. Bridges cannot cross other bridges or islands, must start and end at islands, and always take a single straight, orthogonal line. In most versions, no more than two bridges can connect any two islands. Loops may be permitted in the network.

Where do the bridges run?

Japan
1990AD

SEE ANSWER 193

Nugget number

The largest number that cannot be made by just adding together 0 or more of each of a group of numbers is known as the Frobenius number of that group, after Ferdinand Frobenius, a German mathematician who was active in the late 19th century.

A well-known fast food chain sells adult portions of chicken nuggets in boxes of 6, 9 and 20, co-prime amounts. This inspired Wilson, in 1990, to examine the Frobenius number for chicken nuggets. What is the largest number of nuggets that cannot be purchased?

United States
1990AD

SEE ANSWER 199

THE SIEVE OF CONWAY

John Horton Conway, born on Boxing Day in Liverpool in 1937, is a hugely innovative mathematical discoverer, currently Princeton University's Professor of Mathematics. Among his many other discoveries is Fractran, an 'esoteric' programming language consisting of nothing more than 14 fractions. By running a number through these fractions in a particular pattern, it is possible to generate all the prime numbers that exist, in sequence. This technique has been variously labelled Conway's Prime Producing Machine and The Sieve of Conway.

Take an integer greater than 1 and multiply it by the first fraction. If the result is not an integer, you discard it, and try again with the second fraction. When you finally get a whole number, check if it is a power of 2 – that is, 4, 8, 16, etc. If it is not, repeat the process, using the new number you just got. When you do finally get a number that is a power of 2, the prime number is the value of the power of two that the number is equivalent to. The fractions are:

$^{17}/_{91}$, $^{78}/_{85}$, $^{19}/_{51}$, $^{23}/_{38}$, $^{29}/_{33}$, $^{77}/_{29}$, $^{95}/_{23}$, $^{77}/_{19}$, $^{1}/_{17}$, $^{11}/_{13}$, $^{13}/_{11}$, $^{15}/_{14}$, $^{15}/_{2}$, $^{55}/_{1}$.

So to calculate the first prime number (which is 2, as 1 is generally said not to count), you multiply each of the fractions in turn by 2, until you find one that yields an integer. That's $2 * {^{15}/_2}$, or 15. You then repeat using 15 rather than 2. $15 * {^{55}/_1}$ is 825, not a power of 2. Eventually, you'll get the final result of 4. 4 is 2 to the power of 2, 2^2, so you stop, and the value of the power – 2 – is your prime, which indeed it is.

How many rinses through the sieve does it take to calculate that 2 is prime?

 United States of America
1996AD

SEE ANSWER 195

GOKIGEN NANAME

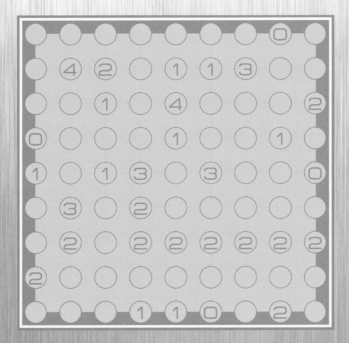

Nikoli's puzzle masters devised Gokigen Naname in 1999.

Each cell in the grid contains one diagonal line from corner to corner. The numbered circles show how many lines touch that corner. The aim is to fill in the grid so that the lines never form a closed circuit of any size. They do not need to form one network, however.

Where are the lines?

Japan
1999AD

SEE ANSWER 198

Fillomino

Fillomino, also known sometimes as Allied Occupation, is a popular Nikoli puzzle created in 2001.

Each value shown in the grid is part of a group of cells. That group has as many cells as the number that is given. A '6' is part of a group of six cells, for example. Groups may take any shape, but no two groups of the same size may touch each other horizontally or vertically at any point, and there are no blank cells. Not all groups are necessarily given a starting value, but some groups may well have more than one of their cells shown at the start.

How are the groups arranged?

Japan
2001AD

SEE ANSWER 197

207

MASYU

A Nikoli creation from 2001, Masyu requires you to join up the dots in a grid.

   A line passes through some or all of the cells in the grid in such a way that it forms a single continuous non-intersecting loop. The line always exits a cell by a different side to the one it entered by, and passes through all cells containing a circle. The line travels straight through a cell with a light circle but turns in the previous and/or following cells in its path. By comparison, the line turns in a cell containing a dark cell, but travels straight through both the previous and following cells in its path.

   Where is the line?

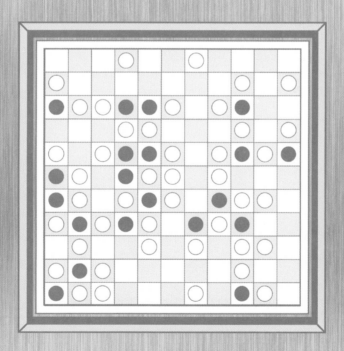

Japan
2001AD

SEE ANSWER 198

Magic Square Matrix

Magic squares are said to be n-order, where n is the number of cells in a row or column. Normal squares hold the numbers 1 to n^2, and each row, column and true diagonal adds to the same number. This constant, M, is always $\frac{(n^3+n)}{2}$. There is only one normal 3-order square (M=15), but there are 880 4-order squares (M=34), almost 300 million 5-order squares (M=65), and so on.

If n is odd, squares can be generated quite easily. Even squares are trickier. There's a reasonably straightforward way to generate squares where n is divisible by four. Squares where n is even but not divisible by 4 are harder. To do these, you need a template n-square of 2x2 blocks, where each block contains the numbers 0 through 3, and each row, column and diagonal on the template adds up to n squared. Then you map each 2x2 block to a single cell of a normal square of order $^n/_2$ (let's call it x), and replace each number in that template block's cell (y) with $x+(y*n^2)$. So a 6-order square will have a template mapped to the 3-order square, and the '1' cell of the 3-order square will generate cells numbered 1, 10, 19 and 28.

Knowing this, can you generate a 6-order square (M=111)?

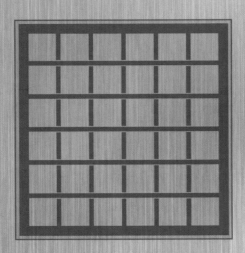

United States of America
2005AD

SEE ANSWER 199

209

NUMBERLINK

Numberlink is one of Nikoli's more recent puzzle innovations, and it too has proven enduringly popular.

Several pairs of numbers or symbols are given in a grid. The player's task is to start at one number and link to its duplicate with one single, continuous line of grid cells. Lines cannot branch, cross each other, or form a knot of cells 2x2 or more. When all the pairs are correctly linked, all of the grid's cells will be filled.

How are the numbers linked?

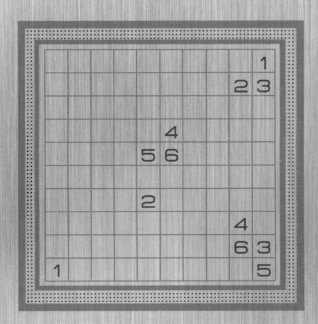

The Ishango Bone

Answer 1. The second side (B) represents the importance of 10 as a number, by omission. 9 and 11, at either end, bracket 10; and 19 and 21, in the centre, bracket 20. Remember that 10 and 20 are very natural human numbers of importance, given our digits. The third side (C) is the most stunning. It gives 11, 13, 17 and 19 – the prime numbers between 10 and 20, in order. The remaining 7 and 5 on the first side extend the sequence of primes to include all the prime numbers below 20 occurring after 4... the first non-prime number.

Holy Days

Answer 2. The two numbers which give a rectangle the same perimeter length and area are 16 and 18. If perimeter = area, then $2(x+y) = x*y$. This is equivalent to $x = 2 + {}^4\!/_{(y-2)}$. For this equation to work, y-2 has to divide into 4 evenly. In other words, y-2 is 1, 2 or 4; and y is 3, 4 or 6, giving respective values of x of 6, 4 and 3. So $6*3 = 6+6+3+3 = 18$, and $4*4 = 4+4+4+4 = 16$. The fact that tabooed 17 falls between these numbers made them all the more magical.

Frustrum

ANSWER 3. Basically, you either know this or you don't, and it turns out the Egyptians did. If h is the height, x is the length of the base and y is the length of the top, then the volume of a truncated pyramid is $h/3*(x^2 + xy + y^2)$. In this case, that's $(4*4 + 4*2 + 2*2) * 2$, or 56. You can get a rough approximation by taking the average of the upper and lower area and multiplying that by the height – that would give you $((16+4)/2) *6$, or 60.

Triangles of Babylon

ANSWER 4. You can either calculate the area of the two triangles, and subtract the larger from the smaller, or work out the area of the trapezoids (height*average length), and multiply that by 3. The latter option is complicated by lack of immediate easy data – we don't know precisely how high the trapezoid is, nor how long the top and bottom lines are. The area of an equilateral triangle of side-length s is $s^2 * {}^{(root\ 3)}/_4$. So for the larger triangle, it's ${}^{25}/_4 *$ root 3, and for the smaller, it's ${}^9/_4 *$ root 3. That's approximately 10.8 - 3.9, or 6.9 square units.

Ahmes' Loaves

ANSWER 5. Ancient Egyptian techniques of division were unwieldy, and you're not expected to be able to guess how they did it. For this puzzle, the trick lies in thinking about the five men getting identical pieces. First off, divide one loaf into 5. That takes care of $1/5$. Divide the remaining two loaves into thirds; that gives you five lots of $1/3$, with an extra $1/3$. Cut the remaining $1/3$ into five pieces, giving you $1/15$s. Then each man gets $1/3 + 1/5 + 1/15$, and Ahmes would have understood exactly what you meant. Note there are infinite other possible answers here, all equivalent and fitting the question – that was one of the flaws of ancient Egyptian fractional technique. To give just one example, you could cut the loaves into 5, 6 and 11, cutting the remaining 6ths and 11ths into 5 in turn, to give $1/5 + 1/6 + 1/11 + 1/30 + 1/55$. Nevertheless, $1/3 + 1/5 + 1/15$ is the most simple solution.

As I was going to Amenemhet III's

ANSWER 6. Nothing too complicated here, just fiddly. Multiplying by 7 each time, we get: 7 houses, 49 cats, 343 mice, 2,401 sheaves of wheat, and 16,807 hekats of grain. Together, that comes to 19,607.

A QUESTION OF QUANTITY

ANSWER 7. Ahmes deals with this problem through *Regula Falsi*. In order to remove the quarter, he starts by assuming that the missing quantity, x, is 4. Then 4 + (4 * 1 / 4) = 5, which is a third of the required sum of fifteen. That means his first guess is three times too small, and x must be 12.

A FRACTIONAL ISSUE

ANSWER 8. In terms of modern mathematics, this question is asking you to find $2/3 + 1/15 + 1/x = 1$. We know now that $2/3$ is equivalent to $10/15$, and 1 to $15/15$, so the answer of $4/15$ is simple. The Egyptians took a different route. First, they multiplied through by the lowest common denominator, 15, to get $10 + 1 + y = 15$, and so y was obviously 4. y is $15*x$, so $x = 1/15*y$, or $4*1/15$. That meant doubling $1/15$ twice, using Ahmes' table. We don't have that, but we can think in multiple fractions instead. Reducing $4/15$ down, the largest unit fraction that we can remove and that leaves a unit fraction behind is $1/5$, leaving $1/15$, so the answer is $1/5 + 1/15$.

Strong grain

ANSWER 9. From our point of view, pesu 10 barley is worth 4.5* pesu 45 barley (from $^{45}/_{10}$), so a fair sum would be 450 hekats. Ahmes gets there by first pointing out that 45 is 35 greater than 10. He then divides that 35 by the 10, to get a unit value of 3 + ½. Then he multiplies this by the 100 hekats for 350 hekats, as the value of the difference, and then adds it back to the original 100 hekats for the total value, getting 450 hekats.

Progressive loaves

ANSWER 10. First of all, you need to work out a standard decrement, or gap, that gives the correct ratio of $^{1}/_{7}$ of the top 3 shares = the bottom 2. You know 5, 4, 3, 2, 1 is wrong, but try it, and you'll find that 3 (from 2+1) - 1 $^{5}/_{7}$ ($^{12}/_{7}$) = 1 $^{2}/_{7}$. Try again with a gap of 2, and you have 9, 7, 5, 3, 1. Now the difference in ratio is 4 - (21 * $^{1}/_{7}$), or 1. The ratio is narrowing, by $^{1}/_{7}$ for every half-point of gap between numbers. We need to get to 0, which means a further three and a half points of gap on from 2 – the first gap to fill the answer is 5 ½. Calculating up from 1, that gives us 1, 6.5, 12, 17.5 and 23, which total to 60. We need them to total to 100, which means multiplying everything by $^{100}/_{60}$, or 1 ⅔. So our final results are 1 ⅔, 10 $^{4}/_{6}$, 20, 29 $^{1}/_{6}$ and 38 ⅓, and the difference between shares is 9 + $^{1}/_{6}$.

DATES

ANSWER 11. Try to answer this problem by reducing the question to fractions and then working it through in the Egyptian style, with only unit fractions, and you'll find it rapidly becomes tryingly complex – particularly without an Egyptian fraction-doubling table to hand. *Regula Falsi* provides a much better approach. Let's try 3, to even out the initial thirds. 3 + 2 is 5, and ⅓ of that is 1 ⅔, leaving 3 ⅓. That's a third of 10, the value we want, so multiple our initial guess by 3, to get 9. 9+6 = 15, and ⅔ of that is 10.

THE RULE OF THREE

ANSWER 12. Simply stated, the Rule of Three is that if we have an equation where a/b = c/x, then by multiplying out, a*x = b*c, and therefore x=b*c/a. Ahmes answers the problem by saying that if the heap was 7 (for easy calculation), then 7 + ($^7/_7$) would be 19. It isn't, it's 8. That means 7 is as far short of the answer as 8 is of 19. So multiplying 7 by the amount required to turn 8 into 19 (which has to be $^{19}/_8$) gives the correct answer – and it does, 16.625 (that .625 is ⅝). Give yourself a bonus point if you broke this down into an Ahmes-friendly 16 + ½ + ⅛. If you're wondering where the Golden Rule comes in, consider the question as $^8/_7$ths of x = 19, or 8x/7=19/1, so 8/7 = 19/x. By the Golden Rule, that then means x = 7 * 19/8.

Progressive Shares

ANSWER 13. Ahmes reasons that the portions must average to 1 (10 hekats / 10 people), and there are only 9 differences between the ten shares. To find where he has to start his sequences (descending), he calculates half of the desired difference, $\frac{1}{16}$, and multiplies that by the 9, to give $\frac{1}{2} + \frac{1}{16}$. Adding this to the average value gives him the largest of the terms, $1 + \frac{1}{2} + \frac{1}{16}$. It is fascinating to realize that this is an exact practical rendering of modern formulae for discovering the largest term of an arithmetic sequence. The smallest, in case you are interested, turns out to be $\frac{1}{4} + \frac{1}{8} + \frac{1}{16}$ of a hekat.

Squaring the Circle

ANSWER 14. The title, here, is the hint. Draw a square of 9*9 that exactly fits the circle, and then divide that square into a three-by-three grid of 9 chunks, each with an area of 9 units sq. You'd get greater accuracy if you divided it into fifths or sevenths than into thirds, but trisecting will do. Look at the grid over the circle, and you'll see that roughly speaking, the circle cuts the corner squares in half, and leaves the other squares intact. If you actually cut the corners in half, producing an octagon, it does follow the circle quite closely. Add up the number of chunks in your octagon, and it comes to 7 pieces of 9 units sq, or 63 units sq. Ahmes fudges the assumption that 63 is almost 64, which is a convenient 8*8, and says that a circle of diameter 9 is equal in area to a square of width 8, and gives the answer as 64*6 = 384. The more obvious answer, from the octagon, is 63*6 = 378, which is what you should have. The modern answer, by the way, is 381.7 – so either way, we're not far out.

SQUARE TRIAL

ANSWER 15. We know that $x^2 + y^2 = 100$. If $y = x*3/4$, then $3x=4y$. The simplest Regula Falsi we can try for the second equation is that x is 4 and y is 3. Putting that into the first equation, we get $16 + 9 = 25$, rather than 100. We are 4 times out, but we can't just multiply x and y by 4, as we're looking at squares. We have to take the square root of 4 to give 2, and multiply by that, so x is 8 and y is 6. Note that the original author, perhaps concerned about cases where the factor isn't a neat square number, instead took the square roots of 25 and 100 (5 and 10 respectively), and observed that they were out by a factor of 2, and derived the 2 that way.

SUMERIAN RIDDLE

ANSWER 16. The riddle refers to a school.

Ramesses' star

ANSWER 17. The knack to this puzzle is continually circling around the star in the same direction, always selecting your previous starting point as your next end point. For example, let's imagine the star's circles are lettered from A to J, starting at the top point and working clockwise around the perimeter line. Then one sequence of moves which will fill 9 spots is as follows: Start at A and jump to D (A>D), then H>A, E>H, B>E, J>B, F>I, C>F, J>C and G>J.

The riddle of the sphinx

ANSWER 18. The answer is man, who crawls when newborn, walks upright when adult, and requires a cane in old age. Oedipus was the one who finally got the riddle right, leading the Sphinx to hurl herself to her death from her lofty perch.

THE QUIET ONE

ANSWER 19. It is a river.

VISITORS

ANSWER 20. The stars.

CRETANS

ANSWER 21. There are several possible approaches. First of all, Epimenides might simply be wrong, in which case there is no paradox. Alternatively, if some Cretans are liars, that can include Epimenides, but not, say, his mother, so he's lying without causing paradox. Or the statement of the paradox itself may itself be a lie; he may have said no such thing. Taking a common sense approach, you can argue that the statement doesn't have to be an absolute and immutable declaration – no-one lies all the time – and thus again, there is no paradox.

ZENO'S DICHOTOMY

ANSWER 22. Zeno is assuming that there are an infinite number of subdivisions of space, but only a finite number of subdivisions of time. Both of these are arbitrary assumptions. Modern molecular physics suggests that space does have a minimum subdivision at the subatomic level, but even discounting that, if space can be infinitely divisible, why not time as well? Then the two infinities cancel out – there may be infinite half-way stages, but it's OK, because you have infinite moments to get to them.

ZENOS' ARROW

ANSWER 23. On one level, it's clear that objects do move, and possess a quality of momentum. But that's not the answer. Interestingly, if you look at reality at the quantum level, it becomes clear that Zeno was absolutely right. If reality is viewed as a purely spatial construct, mediated through a series of time-slices – the classical view of the real world – then there would indeed be no logical point for motion to occur in. Quantum mechanics has shown conclusively that at the subatomic level, if you know an object's position, you cannot know its momentum, and vice versa. In other words, position and momentum are incompatible. If you can say Zeno's Arrow is exactly at point X, then you cannot say it is moving, and vice-versa. It never occurred to Zeno that space and time might be tied together so intimately to form our reality, but his intuition was spot on. If that's not bad enough, consider the Quantum Zeno effect, so named in 1977 – if you watch a Quantum system continuously, its normal passage through time is interrupted. In effect, watching Zeno's arrow that closely actually does make it stand still.

Zeno's Stadium

ANSWER 24. At first glance, Zeno is making the stupid mistake of confusing relative speed with absolute speed. A passes B quickly because B is also in motion. It should be utter rubbish – except that modern physics suggests that if two spaceships approach each other from opposite directions, both travelling at the speed of light, each will appear to the other to be travelling at the speed of light, not twice the speed of light. Looks like Zeno might have a point here after all...

Achilles and the Tortoise

ANSWER 25. As with the Dichotomy, Zeno is discounting the cases where space and time are both equally divisible or indivisible. In either case, it becomes possible for Achilles to meet the Tortoise at exactly the same spot in space–time, and then to pass it. Also, Quantum uncertainty at these super-miniscule distances makes it impossible to talk meaningfully about moving a certain tiny space in a certain tiny time – it can be one or other, but not both.

The heap

ANSWER 26. If you want to retain the notion of the word 'heap' having any meaning, then there has to be an arbitrary point at which the heap stops being a heap, and earns itself some more diminutive adjective. The fact that the word 'heap' doesn't tell us precisely when that occurs is a fault of the vagueness of language, rather than any logical inconsistency. The only alternative positions are that no collection of grains is ever a heap – rather futile, as you can then derive the almost total meaninglessness of language from such a standpoint – or that a single grain can in fact be a heap, which is only a little less unhelpful.

Four brothers

ANSWER 27. The brothers are the four classical elements – water, that runs and runs; fire, that devours; earth, that soaks up moisture; and air, with its howling and whistling.

THE SHOOT

ANSWER 28. The answer is a mountain.

THE NURSERY

ANSWER 29. The riddle refers to a watermelon, with its green skin, white pith, red flesh and seeds.

The Luo River Scroll

ANSWER 30. The Lo Shu is the first magic square, where all straight lines and corner diagonals add up to 15, and opposing pairs of numbers add up to 10. It is the only 3x3 magic square possible.

Buridan's Ass

ANSWER 31. The 17th century Dutch philosopher Spinoza suggested that in fact there was nothing paradoxical about the principle. Unpleasant as it may be, some dilemmas are so convoluted as to lead the victim down a third path of disastrous inactivity, even to the point of death sometimes.

HUI SHI'S THIRD PARADOX

ANSWER 32. This is an issue of relativity, in keeping with Hui Shi's philosophical beliefs. From a viewpoint on a massive scale, the differences between mountain and marsh – or even heaven and earth – are so miniscule as to be non-existent. The obverse, that from a microscopic viewpoint all worldly things are vast, also ties in to some of his other paradoxes. The point is valid; any differentiation only has meaning within a set scale, and so from a certain point of view, any perceived difference is meaningless.

THE ZERO PROOF

ANSWER 33. The flaw in the proof lies in assuming that you can apply the associative law to an infinitely long calculation. Generally, this isn't true. The associative law assumes you have a certain number of terms. Infinity has an uncertain number, so you can't just rearrange the sums. Or look at it this way. Infinity is uncountable, so in both cases, you have infinite pairs of zero terms stretching off. You can either start that chain with a 1 or not, but that doesn't alter the fact that it's the chains themselves that are equal, not the whole expression.

CROCODILE TEARS

ANSWER 34. If the mother says that she will get the baby back, the crocodile is free to eat him and prove her wrong. If she says that the crocodile will eat the baby, and the crocodile does, then it must give the baby back – but if it acknowledges this and gives the baby back, the mother is no longer right, and so the crocodile does not have to give him back after all. This is irreconcilable, and the crocodile may well decide that since both options are impossible, it is free to do as it wishes, and eat the baby – or to gruesomely split the difference. Some thinkers have suggested that the best course is to turn the statement back on the crocodile – so the mother responds, "I predict that if I correctly predict the fate of the my baby, then you will return him. Otherwise, you will eat him." This would unarguably cancel out the crocodile's options, providing that it is taken to count as a valid prediction.

THE LADDER OF HORUS

ANSWER 35. Euclid's formula provides a method of generating Pythagorean triples. If you take two integers, m and n, so that exactly one of them is odd and the two share no common divisors, then the following equations will generate the Pythagorean triples: $x=2mn$, $y=m^2-n^2$, and $z=m^2+n^2$. There are 3 triples with a z of less than 20: 3-4-5, 5-12-13 and 8-15-17.

THE SIEVE OF ERATOSTHENES

ANSWER 36. The sieve's simplicity is breathtakingly elegant. To find all the prime numbers in a range, write them all out starting from 1, and then starting from 2, go through and cross off all the multiples of each uncrossed number. (1 is not generally considered prime). So you do not cross off 2, but cross off 4, 6, 8, 10, 12, etc. 3 is uncrossed, so it is prime, but you cross off 6, 9, 12, 15, etc. 4 is crossed, ignore it, but 5 is uncrossed and prime, and you cross off 10, 15, 20, etc. Go on through to the square root of the number, because any larger divisor must be paired to a smaller divisor. 100 is 25*4, but you'll have hit that possibility at 4 already. 10*10 represents the largest possible smaller divisor. The sieve is so-named because if you write it out as a grid, the primes are the holes.

  Incidentally, the original proof that there is an infinity of primes is as follows: assume that the list of numbers p1, p2, p3 ... p# is the full list of prime numbers. If you multiply all of them together, and then add 1 to the total, you get a new number, P. It is mathematical fact that every non-prime number is a multiple of one or more prime numbers, because only primes are indivisible. So either P is a prime number itself, which makes it a new prime to add to the list, or it is divisible by a prime number that is not already on the list. P cannot be divisible by a prime on the list already, because you got it by multiplying them all together and then adding 1. This would mean that your prime on the list would have to be smaller than 1, which is not allowed. So, in other words, either P is prime, or it is divisible by a prime you don't already know – and there are therefore always more primes.

Archimedes' Revenge

ANSWER 37. This puzzle describes a complex indeterminate polynomial equation that must have an integer solution. The sheer vastness of the numbers concerned makes it extremely difficult. The answer turns out to be 7.76×10^{206544} – a truly gargantuan amount. Number theorists have suggested that if you took a sphere with a diameter equal to the width of our galaxy, and shrunk each of the cattle to the size of an electron, they still wouldn't fit.

The generally accepted text of Archimedes' Revenge has a certain poetic beauty. It goes like this... If thou art diligent and wise, O stranger, compute the number of cattle of the Sun, who once upon a time grazed on the fields of the Thrinacian isle of Sicily, divided into four herds of different colours, one milk white, another a glossy black, a third yellow and the last dappled. In each herd were bulls, mighty in number according to these proportions: Understand, stranger, that the white bulls were equal to a half and a third of the black bulls together with the whole of the yellow bulls, while the black were equal to the fourth part of the dappled and a fifth, together with, once more, the whole of the yellow. Observe further that the remaining bulls, the dappled, were equal to a sixth part of the white and a seventh, together with all of the yellow.

These were the proportions of the cows: The white were precisely equal to the third part and a fourth of the whole herd of the black; while the black were equal to the fourth part once more of the dappled and with it a fifth part, when all, including the bulls, went to pasture together. Now the dappled in four parts were equal in number to a fifth part and a sixth of the yellow herd. Finally the yellow were in number equal to a sixth part and a seventh of the white herd. If thou canst accurately tell, O stranger, the number of cattle of the Sun, giving separately the number of well-fed bulls and again the number of females according to each colour, thou wouldst not be called unskilled or ignorant of numbers, but not yet shalt thou be numbered among the wise.

But come, understand also all these conditions regarding the cattle of the Sun. When the white bulls mingled their number with the black, they stood firm, equal in depth and breadth, and the plains of Thrinacia, stretching far in all ways, were filled with their multitude. Again, when the yellow and the dappled bulls were gathered into one herd they stood in such a manner that their number, beginning from one, grew slowly greater till it completed a triangular figure, there being no bulls of other colours in their midst nor none of them lacking. If thou art able, O stranger, to find out all these things and gather them together in your mind, giving all the relations, thou shalt depart crowned with glory and knowing that thou hast been adjudged perfect in this species of wisdom.

THE NINE CHAPTERS

ANSWER 38. The book presents a fairly sophisticated matrix solution process to answer the puzzle, but it is simpler for us to solve it by algebra. We have three conditions for making one measure, which we can represent as three equations, $2a + b = 1$, $3b + c = 1$ and $4c + a = 1$. This can be solved by substitution. For example, multiply the last equation by 2 to give $8c + 2a = 2$, and subtract this from the first equation, so $2a + b - 8c - 2a = 1 - 2$, or $b - 8c = -1$. This means that $b = 8c - 1$, and we can substitute b in the second equation to get $3(8c-1) + c = 1$, or $25c - 3 = 1$. That gives us $25c = 4$, or $c = 4/25$ths of a measure. Similarly, $b = 7/25$ths and $a = 9/25$ths.

THE CISTERN PROBLEM

ANSWER 39. The first tap provides 48 in 12 hours, or 4/hour. The second tap is twice as fast, so provides 8/hour. The third tap removes 6/hour. The net balance is 6 per hour, so the cistern will fill in 8 hours.

DOG AND HARE

ANSWER 40. We know that a chase of 125pu closes a gap of 50pu. This means that the gap closes 1pu for each 2.5pu chased. So a 30pu gap requires 30*2.5pu to close, or 75pu.

THE CHICKENS

ANSWER 41. Simple algebra will let you solve this puzzle once you've reduced it to appropriate equations. Assuming that the number of purchasers is x, and the actual price is p. Then we know that 9x = p+11, and 6x = p-16. Subtract the latter equation from the former, and 9x - 6x = p + 11 - (p-16), or 3x = 27. So x=9. Then p = 9x - 11, which is 81 - 11, or 70. There are 9 purchasers, paying 70 wen between them.

Leg and Thigh

ANSWER 42. Look at the square inside the triangle, and you'll see that the two smaller triangles it creates are miniature versions of the larger triangle. They share the same angles, and are therefore equivalent, just different sizes. If x is the square's side length, then the sides of one of the smaller triangles on the ku will be ku-x and x in length, not counting the hypotenuse. Because the triangles are equivalent, the ratio of length between the sides must stay the same as in the larger triangle. So ku:kou = (ku-x):x, and x=ku*kou/(ku+kou), or in this case, 60/17 ch'ih.

Men buy a horse

ANSWER 43. The trick here is to represents the men's statements in algebraic form, and then you'll have three simultaneous equations with three unknowns, which is solvable. Noting that they all have whole numbers, the first man has 16 yuan, the second man has 10 yuan, and the third man has 6 yuan.

Greed

ANSWER 44. They're footsteps.

Posthumous Twins

ANSWER 45. The usual answer to this problem is to take the common claimant, the mother, and compare the two children's shares to her share. The ratio of son:mother and mother:daughter is 2:1. The son therefore gets twice as much as the mother, who gets twice as much as the daughter. So the shares are $^4/_7$ to the son, $^2/_7$ to the mother, and $^1/_7$ to the daughter.

The ship of Theseus

ANSWER 46. This is really a philosophical question rather than a simple paradox. Aristotle maintained that it is the form of something that defines its reality, and that the materials used, its content, are of lesser import. In that sense, it is definitely the same ship. Japanese culture assumes this principle as a general fact. In an absolutely rigorous definition of the "same" ship, then no, once one piece is removed, its integrity is violated. Some orthodox Jewish taboos seem to follow this latter view. A utilitarian view might suggest that the ship's final form would have been settled the moment Theseus left it for the last time, and so the first Athenian repair would have invalidated it. In the end though, these are all opinions, and the choice is yours.

MEN FIND A PURSE

ANSWER 47. The lowest sums are 23 in the purse, 9 for the first man, 16 for the second man, and 13 for the third man. Fibonacci finds the answer as follows: "consider the second man. His cash, y, is ½ that of the first man's cash, x, plus the purse's cash, p. The third man's cash, z, is ⅓ (y +p). The first man's is ¼ (z +p). Multiply the fractions of x, y and z, to get a common denominator $^1/_{24}$, and subtract the 1 from the 24 to find the total in the purse, 23. Then to find the total value, he adds 1 to the bottom of each fraction, to give ⅓, ¼ and $^1/_5$, and multiplies through again, for $^1/_{60}$. This time he adds the terms together, to find the total value, 61. He then takes those second fractions, and splits them into pairs, one for each man. He subtracts 1 one from the first of each the pair, multiplies both terms together, and adds them to give each man's share. So ⅓ and ¼ become ½ * ¼, or ⅛, and 1 + 8 is 9 for the first share. ¼ and $^1/_5$ give $^1/_{15}$, or a share of 16, and $^1/_5$ and ⅓ give $^1/_{12}$, or 13". Award yourself a lot of extra points if you used this inductive method rather than something more... sensible.

THE UNWANTED

ANSWER 48. The answer is counterfeit money.

THE FIVE SONS

ANSWER 49. The trick to this puzzle is to convert the requirements into simultaneous equations, and see how many ways it can be solved. For each son, the total number of each type of cask added together will be 9, and when you multiply those numbers by the amount of wine each can hold, they will sum to 18. It turns out that there are eight possible solutions that give 9 casks and 18 pints. You then need five different solutions from that eight that can be added together to give just 9 of each type of cask. This can be done in three different ways. Labelling the types of cask v-z from 4pt to empty for brevity's sake, one brother will always get 3v+w+x+y+3z. The other four will get any two pairs of: (v+3w+2x+y+2z and 2v+w+2x+3y+z), (v+3w+x+3y+z and 2v+w+3x+y+2z), and (v+2w+3x+2y+z and 2v+2w+x+2y+2z)

SUN TZU'S CLASSIC PROBLEM

ANSWER 50. The answer is 23. In general, for each divisor x, you have to find a multiple of the other divisors that is one more than a multiple of x. Call this new multiple a. You then multiply a by the remainder you got after dividing by x, and add this sum to the equivalent figures from the other remainders. If the total is more than your divisors multiplied together, subtract that value and check again. The number remaining is the answer. That produces a unique result for any number of divisors, so long as they are co-prime. So in this puzzle, *3 leaves 2, *5 leaves 3 and *7 leaves 2. The first multiple of 5 * 7 that is 1 greater than a multiple of 3 is 70. Similarly, for *5, it's 21, and for x6, it's 15. (2 * 70) + (3 * 21) + (2 * 15) = 233. Subtract (3 * 5 * 7), or 105, to get 128. Subtract it again to get 23.

THE TROUBLE WITH CAMELS

ANSWER 51. To solve this puzzle, you really need to notice that ½ + ⅓ + ⅑ is $^{17}/_{18}$ths. The lawyer lends a camel to the herd, bringing it to 18 beasts. Then the eldest son gets ½, or 9 camels; the middle son gets ⅓, or 6 camels, and the luckless younger son gets $^{1}/_{9}$, or 2 camels. 9 + 6 + 2 is 17, so the lawyer's camel is still available for him to reclaim.

THE SNAIL AND THE WELL

ANSWER 52. No, the snail will never climb out. The amount it climbs depreciates by 10% a day, so on day two it climbs 1.8 feet, then 1.62, 1.46, 1.31, 1.18, 1.06 and finally, on day eight, 0.95 feet. It loses a foot each night, so if it hasn't made it out by the end of day eight, it may as well give up and enjoy the well. Its maximum height, which falls on day seven, will be the net result of each previous day's climbs (1 + 0.8 + 0.62 + 0.46 + 0.31 + 0.18) + that day's pre-slip climb, 1.06 – a total of 4.43 feet. Close, but not quite close enough.

 Alcuin's Camel

Answer 53. Alcuin's solution is confused, but a proper solution is as follows. If it tries to do the whole first load in one trip, it will arrive with no grain left, unable to get back to the origin. So it must do it in stages. Coming and going is inefficient, because of the camel's feed requirement, so the stages are placed so as to minimise the distance travelled, whilst avoiding abandoning any grain. This puts them at 25% and 50% distance. The first trip, the camel starts with 30 modia of grain and travels to and from the 7.5 league mark, leaving 15 modia there and returning with 0. The second trip, the camel starts with 30 modia again, eats 7.5 to stage 1, replenishes itself back to 30, continues on to stage 2, drops off 7.5 modia, and then uses the remaining 15 going back to the origin. In the final stage, the camel takes the last 30, replenishes the 7.5 it has eaten at stage 1, leaving nothing, and does the same at stage 2. Finally, it travels the last 15 leagues, eating 15 modia, and arriving with 15 modia.

 Brothers and Sisters

Answer 54. Alcuin's solution is optimal. "First of all, my sister and I got into the boat and crossed. Having crossed the river, I let my sister out and recrossed the river. Then the sisters of the two men who remained on the bank got in. When these women had gotten out of the boat, my sister, who had already gone across, got in and brought the boat back to us. She then got out, and the two brothers crossed in the boat. Then, one of the brothers and his sister crossed over to us. However, I and the brother who piloted the boat went across while my sister remained behind. When we had been taken to the [other] side, one of the other women took the boat back across, and my sister came across to us with her at the same time. Then the man whose sister had remained on the other side got in the boat and brought it back with her. Thus the crossing was accomplished, with no one being defiled." Quite.

ALCUIN'S FLASKS

Answer 55. No, it's not possible in this instance. There are five possible solutions, which you can discover by considering the different ways of distributing the full flasks in terms of the way 10 can factor down to three numbers, none greater than 5. Alcuin divides them up into 10 half-full / 5 full 5 empty / 5 full 5 empty. Two solutions give different distributions – 1f 8h 1e / 4f 2h 4e / 5f 0h 5e and 2f 6h 2e / 3f 4h 3e / 5f 0h 5e, but in both cases, one son ends up with no half-full flasks. The remaining two give each son at least one of each, but two sons get the same distribution – 2f 6h 2e / 4f 2h 4f / 4f 2h 4f and 3f 4h 3e / 3f 4h 3e / 4f 2h 4f. Note that the number of full and empty flasks is always the same; this stays true even if the number of flasks varies, and is the reason why when factoring, we can't go above half the total – 6 full means 6 empty, which is more than the allowed share of flasks.

THE EASTERN MERCHANT

Answer 56. Alcuin's answer is to go as far as he can with the most expensive item, and then juggle the rest to reach 100 animals in total. He says, "If you take 10 nine times and add five, you get 95; that is, 19 camels are bought for 95 solidi. Add to this one solidus for an ass, making 96. Then, take 20 times four, making 80 – that is, 20 sheep for four solidi. Add 19 and one and 80, making 100. This is the number of animals. Then add 95 and one and four, making 100 solidi. Hence there are 100 beasts and 100 solidi." Whilst not a general solution for puzzles of this type, it can at least act as a *Regula Falsi* basis for a solution.

ALCUIN'S GRAIN

Answer 57. To start with, the possible maximum numbers are bounded. 6 men, 1 woman and 2 children use up all the grain, as do 1 man, 8 women and 2 children, and 1 man, 1 woman and 30 children. This gives you upper bounds. 2 men would need 18 others, but then 3 women would leave 16 children, and 4 women would leave just 12, so it's not 2 men. 3 men need 17 others, but 1 woman leaves 18 children, and 2 leave 14. With 4 men, it's even worse – right from the start, there are too few people to reach 20. So it has to be 1 man, and by similar elimination, it turns out to be 5 women and 14 children.

THE HUNDRED STEPS

Answer 58. The trick is to notice that taking the top and bottom number together in turn gives a constant value, so that a simple multiplication gives you the answer. In this case, it is simplest to assume there's a zero step as well, and then there are 50 pairs of steps adding up to 100 (100+0, 99+1, etc), down to 51+49. 50 remains as an odd central step. So the answer is 50*100 +50, or 5050.

LCUIN'S RIDDLE

Answer 59. The 'beast' is a comb, which was made of ivory. The two heads refer to the carved ends of the comb, which were in the shape of lions' heads.

HE JOSEPHUS PROBLEM

Answer 60. The most straightforward way to tackle this problem is just to count. The second to last man would have been standing in 16th place.

HE EXPLORER'S PROBLEM

Answer 61. From a starting point of zero, speeds of 10mph and 15mph diverge at a rate of ⅓ of an hour per 10 miles travelled. We need a gap of 2 hours between them, so that's 6*⅓hrs, and 6*10 miles or 60 miles. It takes six hours to do that distance at 10mph, and 4 at 15mph, so sunset is 5 hours away, and the required speed is $^{60}/_5$ or 12mph.

ONKEY NUTS

Answer 62. You can solve this by trial and error, but it is painstaking. A better approach is to convert the four iterations into simultaneous equations with five unknowns: the original total, after the first sailor, after the second sailor, after the third sailor, and in the morning. Reducing these equations down will leave you with a resulting equation in two unknowns, which is much easier to figure out. It helps to realize that each time, the pile that is being hidden must itself be divisible by 3 if the monkey's one coconut is added. The equations you derive can be reduced further, but the answer is that there were 79 coconuts initially.

HE BOOK OF PRECIOUS THINGS

Answer 63. There are 2,678 possible answers to the puzzle, of which Abu Kamil found 2,676 in his Book. One possible solution is 39 ducks, 9 doves, 27 ringdoves, 22 larks and 3 hens, but obviously we can't give them all. To solve the number of answers, assemble the birds into indivisible groups that cost as much as the number of birds they contain. There are five -- (a) 1 hen (1 for 1); (b) 1 duck and 2 doves (3 for 3); (c) 2 ducks, 1 dove and 2 larks (5 for 5); (d) 2 ducks and 3 ringdoves (also 5 for 5); and (e) 3 ducks and 4 larks (7 for 7). The challenge then becomes finding how many ways you can combine these groups to hit 100, which is a more manageable question. You need at least one of (a) and (d), and then at least either one or more of (c) or one or more of both (b) and (e). Note (b) + (e) and (c)+(d) both equal 10 birds, and using these groups, any amount of shortfall can be made up with hens.

A MEDIEVAL RIDDLE

Answer 64. It's an onion, but the riddle is interesting for the earthiness that it displays on the part of the church at the time.

The MARINER

Answer 65. The answer is an anchor.

The Memory Wheel

Answer 66. The wheels are used for generating a full sequence of binary tokens. The smaller wheel represents all possible two-digit tokens, ie. the numbers 0–3, but not in sequence; the larger wheel similarly represents three-digit tokens, the numbers 0–7. Starting from one point, read your two (or three) digits clockwise round the wheel. For the next digit, move clockwise one position. So the small wheel is actually code for 0,0; 0,1; 1,1; 1,0. It is possible to construct memory wheels for an arbitrary number of digits; the number of positions in the wheel will be 1 greater than the maximum number the largest token can describe. The Sanskrit YamAtArAjabhAnasalagAm is actually the same device – it is a nonsense word, with long and short syllables representing binary positions. It can be rendered just as easily as 1000101110, where a short 'a' syllable is a 1 and a long 'A' syllable is a 0. It was used to remember the eight poetic forms, or Ganas, of Sanskrit poetry. The two extra digits, in this instance, are there as duplications of the first two, because the word is not laid out in a circle

Jia Xian's Triangle

Answer 67. A little careful examination should make the ancient Chinese system of Rod Numerals fairly obvious. The Triangle itself is easy to figure out if you start from the top: the nodes in each line are the sum of the nodes feeding into it from the line above. We know this as Pascal's Triangle, and it is a surprisingly powerful and intricate tool for being such a simple construction.

he OLD ONe

Answer 68. The answer is a church bell in a steeple.

he TROUBLE WITh RABBITS

Answer 69. When we start, we have 1 pair. In the first month, the rabbits give birth to a new pair, for 2 pairs. In the second month, just the first rabbits breed again, producing 3 pairs. In the third month, the first new pair also breeds, so we get two more pairs, for a total of 5. In the fourth month, we have three breeding pairs, for a total of 8 – and so on for 13, 21, 34, 55, 89, 144, 233 and finally 377. The pattern 1, 1, 2, 3, 5, 8, 13, ... should be familiar: it is the Fibonacci Sequence, named for Fibonacci, who set the puzzle in the *Liber Abaci*. It is one the best-known mathematical sequences, and finds expression throughout nature, art and science.

 The RING Game

Answer 70. Through the multiplications, the different elements of the answer – seat number, finger number and joint number – are put into separate digits of the final total. Take away 350, the base value of the first set of multiplications, and the digits of the result give you seat, finger and joint. For example, someone in the 8th seat, with a ring on the 2nd joint of finger 4, will result in a total of 8*2 = 16, +5 = 21, *5 = 105, +10 = 115. (115 + 4) * 10 = 1190, and +2 = 1192. 1192-350 = 842, which breaks back down to 8 - 4 - 2.

 The Well

Answer 71. Fibonacci uses *Regula Falsi* to derive the answer to this puzzle. First he points out that from the top of each tower to its base to the well and back up to the tower top is an equilateral triangle. The birds arrive at the same time, so the length of the hypotenuse in both triangles is the same. Assuming that the taller tower is 'A' paces from the well and the shorter is 'Z', then from Pythagoras's Theorem, we know that $A^2 + 40^2 = Z^2 + 30^2$. To solve this, he says, suppose A is 10, making Z 40. Then that side of the equation will be 100 + 1600 (1700), and the other side will be 1600 + 900 (2500). That's an erroneous imbalance of 800. Try again with A=15 and Z=35. Now we get 1825 = 2125, which is an imbalance of 300. We have increased A by 5 and found that we are 500 closer to our answer. We need to be 300 closer still, so increase A by 3. A=18 and Z=32 gives us 1924 on both sides. The well is 18 paces from the taller tower.

# ARTAGLIA'S WINE

Answer 72. There isn't any general solution to this problem, but rendering the limits of the jugs as a graph and exploring and moving from boundary node to boundary node can help. Anyhow. The optimal answer is to take the following steps: Fill the 3pt jug, empty it into the 5pt jug, fill the 3pt jug from the 8pt jug again, then fill the 5pt jug from 3pt jug. This gives you 1pt in the 3pt jug, 5pt in the 5, and 2pts in the 8. Empty the 5pt jug into the 8pt and empty the 1pt into the 5pt, giving you 0, 1 and 7pts. Then fill the 3pt from the 7pt, and empty the 3pt into the 5pt. Now both 5 and 8 contain 4pts.

# OPSY-TURVY

Answer 73. The answer is actually trickier for us to hit on nowadays than it would have been originally – it's a nail in a (horse)shoe.

The Wanderer

Answer 74. It is a needle and thread.

The hound

Answer 75. The answer is a shoe.

Regiomontanus Angle

Answer 76. If you draw a circle passing exactly through the top and bottom points of the painting, so that it just touches the eye-level line at one tangential point, that spot where the circle meets the eye-level line is the point of maximum angle width. The distance of this spot from the wall is equal to the square root of the sum of the squares of the height of the top and bottom of the painting.

The Problem of Points

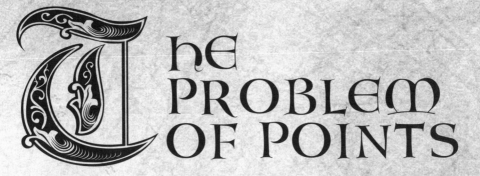

Answer 77. Pacioli's answer, to split the pot according to the number of rounds won up to then, is problematic. What if the game is interrupted after just one or two rounds? It wasn't until Pascal and Fermat started discussing the issue in the 17th century that a good solution was found. The answer is that the division of the pot must depend on the different probable outcomes of the game at that point, rather than on any detail of its history. By working out all the possible remaining outcomes, and tallying which fall to which player, it becomes possible to fairly divide the pot. If one player is 95% certain to win, that player should get 95% of the spoils. A lot of modern probability theory derives from Pascal's and Fermat's work on this puzzle.

Modesty

Answer 78. The riddle refers to a walnut.

URER'S SQUARE

Answer 79. Amazingly, there are 13 different ways to divide the square into four groups of four numbers that sum to 34. These are:

1. Rows,
2. Columns,
3. Diagonals (the numbers orthogonally adjacent to opposing corner squares are the other two groups in this set),
4. Dividing the square into quarters,
5. Taking the top or bottom half of each such quarter with the same section of the quarter below it,
6. Taking the left or right half of each quarter with the same section of the quarter next to it,
7. Taking the top half of each quarter with the bottom half of the quarter diametrically opposed to it,
8. Taking the left half of each quarter with the right half of the quarter diametrically opposed to it,
9. Taking the same cell from each of the four quarters,
10. Taking the same cell from the top two quarters with its diametrically opposed cell in the bottom two quarters,
11. Taking the same cell from the leftmost two quarters with its diametrically opposed cell in the rightmost two quarters,
12. Taking cells clockwise or anti-clockwise from the quarters in turn as you progress clockwise around them (but to make it trickier, the groups starting top left and bottom right in the top left quarter rotate anticlockwise as you progress, but the other two rotate clockwise), and
13. Taking the central four cells (and the groups of four numbers remaining horizontally, vertically and diagonally).

 An Odd Gift

Answer 80. The traditional answer is that it is your word.

 Clock Striking Problem

Answer 81. A clock marking the hours will strike 90 times from the first stroke of midday to the last stroke of midnight (or vice versa)

HE DINNER PARTY

Answer 82. If you had a third numeric detail about the men, women and children, you could turn this into a problem of simultaneous equations. As it is, you can reduce one of the terms, and use trial and error on the remaining terms to find the answer. There are 5 men, 3 women and 33 children.

RICKING THE LANDLORD

Answer 83. The simplest approach to this is *Regula Falsi* – start with the landlord first, and then work round to see who is left. Once you know the relative positions of start and end point, it's easy to rotate that round so that the landlord is left. Counting clockwise, with the landlord in position 22, the first person you count should be number 6.

OUND AND ROUND

Answer 84. The solution is the sun.

ACHET'S SCALES

Answer 85. The key to this problem is to think of the possible states that a scale can be in – tipped left, balanced and tipped right. This gives you three possible states. To account for these states, you need to spread your weights in powers of 3. So weights of 1, 3, 9 and 27 are all you need to balance any weight of up to 40, their combined total. For some loads, you'll need to add weights to both sides of the scale, but that is perfectly reasonable. In general, a set of ternary weights like this will allow you to measure up to 150% of the heaviest single weight.

UPERT'S CUBE

Answer 86. Oddly enough, if you cut your hole across a slanted diagonal of your original cube, you can actually fit a larger cube through it. The maximum size turns out to be ¾ (root 2) – or 1.06 – times the original.

The NEWTON-Pepys Problem

Answer 87. Pepys' intuitive suspicion was that the largest roll was the easiest. It's not the case, though. You are more likely to make the six-die roll. Newton pointed our that you could imagine the 12-die roll as two sets of the 6-die roll, and the 18-die roll as three sets. To make the 6-die set, you only have to achieve success once. The other sets effectively require you to make the roll more than once. The relative probabilities aren't that simple – you can roll more than 3 sixes in the 18-die roll, at which point you can't quite keep the principle holding true. The 6-die roll has a 0.66 chance, the 12-die roll a 0.62 chance, and the 18-die roll a 0.60 chance.

Sunday

Answer 88. They are going to a funeral. The four men are the pall-bearers; the fifth man is the deceased, in a coffin.

The TOURIST

Answer 89. The traditional answer is a watch.

The BRIDGES OF KONIGSBERG

Answer 90. Euler reasoned that in any network of linked points (usually now known as a graph), each point (node) must either be connected by an even number of lines or an odd number of lines. If you are to be able to walk each line and return to where you started (a 'closed Euler walk'), then you must be able to leave every node you enter – in other words, every node must be even. If you accept starting in one node and ending in a different one, an open Euler walk, there must be exactly two nodes which are odd. If you look at the bridges as a graph, you'll see that there are four nodes (north bank, south bank, big island and small island), and all four have an odd number of lines. No Euler walk is possible.

WALKING THE WALK

Answer 91. In general, the way to find an open Euler walk if you know one is there is to start at a point, move to another by an unused line, and keep going until you run out of room to progress. Then look back over your progress. Somewhere, there will be a node that has an exit you haven't already used. Go back to that and start a new walk, using only lines you have not already used, then splice the new walk into the previous walk. Repeat until the whole graph is covered, and you will have a single composite walk. There are obviously lots of different ways of making a Euler walk in a figure this complex, but one would be as follows: A-D-I-K-J-A-B-C-B-H-C-D-F-I-H-K-F-E-H-G-J-E-A-G.

THE TETHERED GOAT

Answer 92. The goat will be able to move within an oval area bounded by the fence on one side and the radius of its own rope on the other. If the rope is the same radius as the field, the goat will get to the centre of the field, but then be pulled away from the top and bottom. To compensate, and give it enough slack to get to half the area of the field, the rope needs to be longer. (As a point of interest, it needs to be 1.16 the length of the radius of the field).

UFFON'S NEEDLE

Answer 93. The chance of any given needle toss crossing a seam depends largely on the angle (x) that the needle makes to the horizontal. The closer the needle to perpendicular, the longer it will seem relative to the perpendicular gap between the lines. This effective length is the sine of the angle of the needle, so solving the specific question of each angle's chance requires solving $\sin(x)$. Without getting into the maths too much, sine waves are fundamentally derived from circular motion through time, and Buffon's problem requires the use of pi in order to solve the sine function. In simpler terms, because the angle of the needle varies, the point of the needle effectively becomes a point on a circle (imagine a coin landing between the seams), and this brings pi into the mix, from where it can then be worked out once you know the probability.

HE THUNDERER

Answer 94. The riddle refers to a shotgun.

THE MINER

Answer 95. The answer is graphite, pencil lead.

THE BLIND ABBOT

Answer 96. So long as the monks leave the centre cells of each row empty, they can distribute nine people in one linked pair of corner cells as they wish, and then use the same pattern, reversed, for the other pair of cells. So, for example, they could have 5 people top left and bottom right, and 4 top right and bottom left. However they arrange it, there are nine in each row, and only 18 of the 24 accounted for. When it comes to smuggling the girls in, the trick is to empty the corner cells and put nine people in each centre cell, for a total of 36.

THE CAPTIVE QUEEN

Answer 97. The puzzle is reminiscent of Alcuin's River Crossing, in that multiple journeys back and forth are required. First one basket is pulled up, and the stone dropped in. It sinks, and the empty basket comes up. The son gets in, and the stone returns. The daughter takes the stone out and gets in, and sinks to the ground, returning the son to the top. Both daughter and son get out, the son puts the stone in, and the empty basket returns. The daughter then gets in with the stone at the bottom, and the queen gets in at the top, lowering the queen and raising the daughter and the stone. Both the daughter and the queen get out, and the stone drops, leaving the empty basket with the son and daughter at the top, and the stone with the queen at the bottom. The son gets in again, and drops, raising the stone. The daughter replaces the stone with herself, and drops down, raising her brother. The son and daughter both get out. Now the queen and her daughter are at the bottom, and the son and the stone are at the top. The son puts the stone in, which drops, and then gets in the empty basket. He drops to the ground and gets out to join his family. Finally, the stone crashes back to earth again as the queen and her children leave.

SPIRAL WALK

Answer 98. The area of a rectangle is width * height, and this is going to equal the area of the path, 3630*1 yards. As height = width + 0.5, then width (x) becomes x * (x+0.5) = 3630, or $x^2 + x*0.5 = 3630$. The highest square number under 3630 is 3600, the square of 60 – and half 60 is 30. So the garden is 60 yards wide.

EIGHT QUEENS

Answer 99. There are a dozen unique solutions to the problem – and almost 4.5 billion different possible arrangements of the eight queens. There is a general solution for placing X queens on an X by X board, as long as X is more than 4. First of all, divide X by 12 and remember the remainder (Z). In our puzzle, that's still 8. Write down all the even numbers between 1 and X in order, but if Z is 3 or 9, move 2 to last place. Now follow this with all the odd numbers between 1 and X in order, except that if Z is 8, take the numbers in pairs, and swap their order – so 3, 1, 7, 5, etc. Then, if Z is 2, switch the positions of 1 and 3, and move 5 to the end of the list or, if Z is 3 or 9, move 1 and 3 to the end of the list. Now the list of numbers you have gives the row number of each queen as you place it in turn from 1 to X. For this puzzle, that gives us a list of 2, 4, 6, 8, 3, 1, 7, 5, and queens at 2a, 4b, 6c, 8d, 3e, 1f, 7g, and 5h. Of course, you might have arrived at one of the other 11 solutions manually, but this is the easiest way to do it once you know how.

THE DINNER PARTY

Answer 100. There is just one guest. The Governor has a brother and a sister, who are themselves married to a sister and brother pair. He also has a wife, who has no siblings. All six of them are grandchildren of the same couple – that is, they are all first cousins. The Governor's father has a brother, who is the father of the governor's wife, and a sister, who is the mother of the governor's siblings' spouses. It is to be hoped that the Governor's father and his siblings married spouses from separate families! Note also that marriage between first cousins, whilst not particularly advisable on genetic grounds, is not generally illegal.

THE MONKEY AND THE PULLEY

Answer 101. Imagine the monkey is suddenly one yard higher. Because it is then nearer to the pulley than the weight is, the force of the monkey's mass has greater moment, and the monkey will sink back down again until the two weights are balanced. In other words, as the monkey climbs, the weight will rise with it – half of the monkey's effort will go to lifting it, and the other half to lifting the weight.

KIRKMAN'S SCHOOLGIRLS

Answer 102. There are fifteen girls, so for each individual schoolgirl, there are 14 other girls, who can thus be arranged in seven pairs. So it is possible, yes. The generalised mathematical method for reaching a solution is quite arcane – the puzzle represents a combinatorial Steiner Triple with parallelism – but there are seven possible group arrangements (which can obviously be shuffled around different days at will). One such solution, if the girls are lettered A - O, would be:

ABC, DEF, GHI, JKL, MNO;
AFI, BLO, CHJ, DKM, EGN;
ADH, BEK, CIO, FLN, GJM;
AGL, BDJ, CFM, EHO, IKN;
AEM, BHN, CGK, DIL, FJO;
AJN, BIM, CEL, DOG, FHK; and
AKO, BFG, CDN, EIJ, HLM.

HE COUNTERFEIT BILL

Answer 103. Whilst it is tempting to say that the hatter has lost $10, this isn't strictly true. The price of the hat includes a profit margin, p, which we don't know. The hatter hasn't lost p, because he never had it in the first place. So he has lost $10-p or, to put it another way, the cost of replacing the hat plus the $3.70 in change he handed over.

HE TRAVELLING SALESMAN

Answer 104. Unlike Euler graphs, there is no easy way to tell for sure whether a Hamilton graph has a solution or not. You just have to examine the graph and explore the possibilities. In this case, no, there is no Hamilton route.

ETHIOPIAN MATHEMATICS

Answer 105. The Ethiopian system is actually a highly sophisticated physical implementation of binary, the system computers work in. The second column, dividing the $22 value of each bull by two until 1 is reached, is in fact just calculating the binary equivalent of the number. Working from the first hole down, if stones means 1 and no stones means 0, we get 10110, which is 22 in binary. Each digit in binary is one of the powers of two (1, 2, 4, 8, etc), where 1 means 'include that' and 0 means 'don't include' -- so 10110 is 16 + (not 8) + 4 + 2 + (not 1). If the second column is calculating the binary value for a number, then the first column is just a handy way of multiplying that number. By starting from the unit value, 7, and then doubling, each column becomes 7* that binary digit. 14 is 7*2, 28 is 7*4, and so on. Because 22 is 10110, 7*22 is (not 7*1) + 7*2 + 7*4 + (not 7*8) + 7*16, and adding those stones gives you your final answer. The system will always work – for whole numbers, anyway.

CANTOR'S INFINITIES

Answer 106. It turns out that the notion of 'larger' has to be broadly discarded at infinity. On the one hand, the natural numbers are trivially twice as numerous as the even numbers. On the other hand, both sets are trivially infinite, and therefore the same size. It gets worse, though. For any given set, there is a Power set, which consists of all of the possible subsets derived from that set, and it is easily provable that a Power set is considerably larger than its original set. So what about the Power set of the natural numbers? Cantor's answer was to describe different levels of infinity in terms of their relative countability – the natural numbers and the even numbers are both countable, and thus are at the lowest ordinal rank of infinity, known as Aleph Null. If a set contains N items, its Power set contains 2^N items – Cantor described this as the first level of uncountable infinity, Aleph One. Cantor's work on infinity is startlingly beautiful, even spiritual in some odd senses – he himself believed it was told to him by God – and is well worth a closer look than the very, very brief treatment given here.

 OBODY

Answer 107. The riddle refers to tomorrow, which never truly comes.

 ESSERACT

Answer 108. On the tesseract map given, any four numbers in one quadrilateral shape add up to 34, and, taken clockwise, give a line of a magic square. The other three quadrilateral planes parallel to that one in the map give you the other lines of the square. So starting top left with the simple square 13-2-7-12, the squares 3-16-9-6, 10-5-4-15 and 8-11-14-1 complete the rows of a 4-order square.

 ERTRAND'S
BOX

Answer 109. The intuitive assumption is that the chance is ½. You've picked one gold, so the box was either GG or GS, and you have either G or S left. This is wrong. The mistake is in forgetting that each box holds two coins, and therefore gives you two possible pathways. The two golds in GG may be the same functionally, but they are very different probabilistically. Let's rename GG as g1g2, and leave the GS pair as GS. You may have G, in which case the other coin is S, you may have g1, in which case it is g2, or you may have g2, in which case it is g1. So there are three possibilities, and two of them are gold; the possibility is ⅔. This is the foundation of a card scam using the same set-up (with blank cards colour-marked on both sides). The scammer offers a 2–1 return on a different colour when the selected card is flipped, knowing the odds are ⅔, and he'll win big in the long run.

 OTHING LOST

Answer 110. The digits from 9 down to 1 sum up to 45. If you arrange them in order as two nine digit numbers, 987654321 and 123456789, you can subtract the lesser from the greater to leave a nine-digit number that itself uses each of the digits from 1 to 9 once, 864197532. Summing each of the numbers in your calculation, all three will add to 45.

 ILBERT'S HOTEL

Answer 111. There is no limit to numbers in infinity. Although the hotel already has an infinite number of guests, filling an infinite number of rooms, VALIS can transport each current guest to the room whose number is twice their current room number. That frees up all the odd numbers, of which there are an infinite number, and the new arrivals can be jaunted in. Note that that's not the only way that the room space can be expanded; VALIS could move everyone up one space, book the next guest in, and repeat infinitely. Of course, that would take infinitely long...

Because it is so counter-intuitive – but totally accurate – some thinkers (often religious ones) have taken Hilbert's Hotel to imply the non-existence of infinity.

INE/WATER PROBLEM

Answer 112. It is easy to see the solution to this when you think about the fact that the total volume of liquid in the two barrels must be conserved. Wine and water displace equal amounts of each other, so any amount of wine polluting the water must be equalled by an identical amount of water in the wine. The two mixtures are of equal purity.

HE BARBER PARADOX

Answer 113. No clear logical solution exists to the problem; it is inherently self-contradictory. One possible get-out is that the barber shaves himself, but only in his capacity as a private citizen, not whilst he is on duty as the barber. Russell himself noted that if you reduce the question to the underlying mathematics of set theory, it is inherently meaningless, and therefore no logical solution can be expected.

AMMA'S AGE

Answer 114. The age of Mamma must have been 29 years 2 months; that of Papa, 35 years; and that of the child, Tommy, 5 years 10 months. Added together, these make seventy years. The father is six times the age of the son, and, after 23 years 4 months have elapsed, their united ages will amount to 140 years, and Tommy will be just half the age of his father.

PAPA'S PROBLEM

Answer 115. The intuitive answer – that if you cut ⅓ of the way along, the area of the remaining triangle will be the same as the remaining square third – will not work. The extra moment of force from the elongated side has to be taken into account. Dudeney says that the correct ratio of the balance point along the long side turns out not to be ⅓ to ⅔, but 1 to (root 3), equivalent to multiplying the length by 0.366 to find the balance point. He provides a practical proof: place your cardboard on a larger sheet of paper, and draw an equilateral triangle with base equal to the base of the card, overlapping and extending above the card. Mark a position from one of the upper corners of the card as far in as the card is high (squaring the shorter side). Then take the diagonal of that square, and extend it out above the card to the edge of the equilateral triangle. The point where it intersects the triangle edge is, when drawn straight back down to the base, the point of balance. Note that this balance point is independent of the height of the card.

KITE PROBLEM

Answer 116. Dudeney points out that the volume of a sphere of diameter X is equal to that of a circular cylinder of X diameter and two-thirds X in height. In other words, the cylinder equivalent would be 16" tall, and 24" diameter. This can then be seen as a myriad of 16" wire circles packed together into the cylinder. The ratio of the area of two circles is in proportion to the ratios of the squares of their diameters. The square of $\frac{1}{100}$ (the diameter of the wire) is $\frac{1}{1000}$, and the square of 24 is 576, so the number of wire 'circles' that can fit in the cylinder is 5,760,000. Each wire is 16" long, so the wire would be a massive 92,160,000" long, or 1,454 miles and 2,880 feet – a mile is 1,760 yards long.

The Barrel of Beer

Answer 117. We know that we need to add all the barrels to a total divisible by three with one left over. The total of all six is 119. That's not divisible by three, so removing 15 or 18 would be no help. Further more, 119 is two above 117, the previous number divisible by three, so subtracting a number that is just 1 above being divisible by three – i.e. 31, 19 and 16 – is also no use. The only barrel that is 2 numbers above a multiple of 3 is 20, so that is the beer. Remove that, and you have 99 left, divided into 66 to one man and 33 to the other.

The Century Puzzle

Answer 118. You can go a fair way towards eliminating impossible options for this puzzle with digital root theory, and some first-principle deductions will help, such as being unable to use numbers with repeated digits. However, the problem remains quite challenging. The answer is $3 + {}^{69258}/_{714}$.

The Labourer's Puzzle

Answer 119. The man is going twice as deep as he has done so far, so when finished, the hole will be three times its present depth. We know that when depth D = 3D, then head height H = -2H, and that D < 5ft 10, and 3D > 5ft 10 and 3D < 11ft 8. Therefore D can only be 3ft 6 (so H is 2ft 4), and when finished, H will be -4ft 8 and D will be 10ft 6.

FENCE PROBLEM

Answer 120. Like Dudeney says, "One is scarcely prepared for the fact that the field, in order to comply with the conditions, must contain exactly 501,760 acres, the fence requiring the same number of rails. Yet this is the correct answer, and the only answer, and if that gentleman in Iowa carries out his intention, his field will be twenty-eight miles long on each side. I have, however, reason to believe that when he finds the sort of task he has set himself, he will decide to abandon it; for if that cow decides to roam to fresh woods and pastures new, the milkmaid may have to start out a week in advance in order to obtain the morning's milk."

PIERROT'S PUZZLE

Answer 121. There are just six ways of doing this in total. The initial 15 * 93 = 1395, plus 9 * 351 = 3159, 21 * 87 = 1287, 27 * 81 = 2187, 8 * 473 = 3784, and 35 * 41 = 1436.

THE FOUR SEVENS

Answer 122. The only way to do it is to use a bit of cheek, and imply a couple of non-available 0s. (7/.7) * (7/.7) works out at 10*10, or 100. This works for any number, of course; x/(x/10) is the same as x * (10/x), which cancels out to give you 10.

R. GUBBINS IN THE FOG

Answer 123. The candles must have burnt for three hours and three-quarters. One candle had one-sixteenth of its total length left and the other four-sixteenths.

HE BASKET OF POTATOES

Answer 124. Dudeney states that to find the distance, you should multiple together the number of potatoes (p) by (p-1) and (2p-1), and then divide by 3. 50, 49 and 99 multiply together for 242,550, which is 3 times 80,850 yds – or almost 46 miles.

HE LOCKERS

Answer 125. The smallest total you can get in the hundreds column is going to be 2 + 1 = 3. That leaves you a minimum tens column of 0 + 4 =5, achieved by having 7 + 9 = 16 in the last column, giving you 107 + 249 (although obviously each digit could be swapped by its counterpart in the previous line as you see fit) = 356. The highest total, by similar logic, must have 9 in the hundreds column, and you can contrive it to have 8 in the tens column, with numbers summing to 7 above it. The highest possible combination here is 245+736 (or an equivalent counterpart)=981. This leaves you the digits 0, 2, 4 and 7 for the sum of the central cupboard. There are three possible sums, 134 + 568 = 702, 134 + 586 = 720, and 138 + 269 = 407.

ODD MULTIPLICATION

Answer 126. The answer is that 32,547,891 * 6 = 195,287,346, and congratulations if you discovered it.

CURIOUS NUMBERS

Answer 127. It's not an easy problem to solve without some computing assistance. As Dudeney says, the next three numbers after 48 are 1,680, 57,120 and 1,940,448. You could probably arrive at 1,680 with some trial and error but if you got the other two, you've done well indeed – even if you thought to use a computer program!

CHANGING PLACES

Answer 128. Dudeney points out that there are thirty-six pairs of times when the hands exactly change places between three p.m. and midnight. The number of pairs of times from any hour (n) to midnight is the sum of the first (12-n+1) natural numbers. In the case of the puzzle n = 3; therefore 12 - (3 + 1) = 8 and 1 + 2 + 3 + 4 + 5 + 6 + 7 + 8 = 36, the required answer. The first pair of times is 3h 21 $^{57}/_{143}$m and 4h 16 $^{112}/_{143}$m, and the last pair is 10h 59 $^{83}/_{143}$m and 11h 54 $^{138}/_{143}$m. He gives the following formula by which any of the sixty-six pairs that occur from midday to midnight may be at once found, if (a) is an hour, and (b) is a different, later hour: (720b+60a/143) mins after a, and (720a+60b/143) mins after b. From these equations, you can find that the time nearest 45m is at 11h 44 $^{128}/_{143}$m, which is paired to 8h 58 $^{106}/_{143}$m.

THE NINE COUNTERS

Answer 129. Because only one of the four numbers involved is three-digit, it should be reasonably clear that the hundreds digit needs to be low, and the tens digits of the other multiplication will need to be high. Even so, you'll need a certain amount of patience to get to the answer, but 174 * 32 = 96 * 58 = 5568.

DONKEY RIDING

Answer 130. The third and fourth quarters are equal, and equal to the total of the first and second quarters, so the time for the first three quarters is ¾ of the total time. 6.75/0.75 gives 9 minutes.

The Spot on the Table

Answer 131. Dudeney says, "The ordinary schoolboy would correctly treat this as a quadratic equation. Here is the actual arithmetic. Double the product of the two distances from the walls. This gives us 144, which is the square of 12. The sum of the two distances is 17. If we add these two numbers, 12 and 17, together, and also subtract one from the other, we get the two answers that 29 or 5 was the radius, or half-diameter, of the table. Consequently, the full diameter was 58 in. or 10 in. But a table of the latter dimensions would be absurd, and not at all in accordance with the illustration. Therefore the table must have been 58 in. in diameter. In this case the spot was on the edge nearest to the corner of the room — to which the boy was pointing. If the other answer were admissible, the spot would be on the edge farthest from the corner of the room."

Catching the Thief

Answer 132. The constable took thirty steps. In the same time the thief would take forty-eight, which, added to his start of twenty-seven, carried him seventy-five steps. This distance would be exactly equal to thirty steps of the constable.

HAT WAS THE TIME?

Answer 133. *Regula Falsi* works nicely for this puzzle. Say it's 8pm. Then a quarter of the time from noon is 2hrs, and a half of the time to the following noon is 8hrs. The total is 2hrs too much. Try 9pm, giving you 2.25hrs before and 7.5hrs after. That's 9.75hrs, or 45 minutes too much. So an hour extra is worth 1.25hrs. You need to decrease the gap by .75 hrs. 0.75/1.25 is 0.6, or 36 minutes. The time is 9.36pm. A quarter of the time from noon is 2h 24m, and half the time to next noon is 7h 12m, or 9h 36m.

HE THIRTY-THREE PEARLS

Answer 134. The big pearl must be worth £3,000. The pearl on one end is worth £1,400, and on the other end £600.

The Three Villages

Answer 135. The villages A, B, C form a triangle. The line from B to a point on AC (let's call it O) is 12 miles, and forms a square angle. So we also have two right-angled triangles, OBA and OBC, where OB is 12. We know that the sides are all exactly whole numbers, and that the two hypotenuses AB and BC are 35 in total, and unequal, so OB has to be the longer side of OBA and the shorter side of OBC. The simplest Pythagorean triple, (3, 4, 5), is a good place to start, indicated by OB's length of 12 being divisible by both 3 and 4. If 12 is the longer (4) side of OBA, then each other length is multiplied by 3, and OA is 3*3 (9) and AB is 3*5 (15). Similarly, for OBC, the lengths are *4, to give OC as 4*4 (16) and BC as 5*4 (20). AB + BC = 15 + 20 = 35, so we're right, and the distances are AB=15, BC=20 and AC=9+16=25.

Eternal

Answer 136. The letter 'e'.

The Village Simpleton

Answer 137. It's Sunday. If the day after tomorrow is yesterday, that's three days in the future; if the day before yesterday is tomorrow, that's three days in the past. The only way that three days either way can be equidistant from Sunday is if today is Sunday.

W HAPSHAW'S WHARF MYSTERY

Answer 138. As Dudeney says, "There are eleven different times in twelve hours when the hour and minute hands of a clock are exactly one above the other. If we divide 12 hours by 11 we get 1 hr. 5 min. 27 $^3/_{11}$ sec., and this is the time after twelve o'clock when they are first together, and also the time that elapses between one occasion of the hands being together and the next. They are together for the second time at 2 hr. 10 min. 54 $^6/_{11}$ sec. (twice the above time); next at 3 hr. 16 min. 21 $^9/_{11}$ sec.; next at 4 hr. 21 min. 49 $^1/_{11}$ sec. Keep going, and you will find that this last is the only occasion on which the two hands are together with the second hand just past the forty-ninth second. This, then, is the time at which the watch must have stopped."

THE SPIDER AND THE FLY

Answer 139. If the spider travels orthogonally, the distance to the fly is 42 feet – 11 feet to the floor, 30 feet to the other wall, and 1 foot back up. A shorter distance can be found if you flatten the room out into a 2-D construction template, with one end wall attached to the ceiling space, and the other to the floor space. A straight line between these two points on the template corresponds to a diagonal path across ceiling, wall and floor, and its length is just 40 feet.

CIRCLING THE SQUARES

Answer 140. Dudeney says, "The squares that are diametrically opposite have a common difference. For example, the difference between the square of 14 and the square of 2, in the diagram, is 192; and the difference between the square of 16 and the square of 8 is also 192. This must be so in every case. Then it should be remembered that the difference between squares of two consecutive numbers is always twice the smaller number plus 1, and that the difference between the squares of any two numbers can always be expressed as the difference of the numbers multiplied by their sum. Thus the square of 5 (25) less the square of 4 (16) equals (2 × 4) + 1, or 9; also, the square of 7 (49) less the square of 3 (9) equals (7 + 3) × (7 - 3), or 40. Now, the number 192, referred to above, may be divided into five different pairs of even factors: 2 × 96, 4 × 48, 6 × 32, 8 × 24, and 12 × 16, and these divided by 2 give us, 1 × 48, 2 × 24, 3 × 16, 4 × 12, and 6 × 8. The difference and sum respectively of each of these pairs in turn produce 47, 49; 22, 26; 13, 19; 8, 16; and 2, 14. These are the required numbers, four of which are already placed. The six numbers that have to be added may be placed in just six different ways, one of which is as follows, reading round the circle clockwise: 16, 2, 49, 22, 19, 8, 14, 47, 26, 13."

CHARLEY AND MISS LOFTY

Answer 141. "Mr. Lightop," replied the offended maiden, "I presume you claim that there is a man in both, but opinions might differ on that subject."

 CAST ASHORE

Answer 142. The ship is the Ark, and the note's author Noah.

 THE BANK OF MONTE CARLO

Answer 143. There are 6*6*6 different possible outcomes of the dice, giving 216 possibilities. Die 1 wins with a $\frac{1}{6}$ chance. If it loses, die 2 wins with a $\frac{5}{6} * \frac{5}{6}$ chance. If that loses too, die 3 wins with a $\frac{5}{6} * \frac{5}{6} * \frac{1}{6}$ chance. Multiply each of those out, putting them in terms of fractions of 216, and the total chance of a win is $\frac{36}{216} + \frac{30}{216} + \frac{25}{216}$, or $\frac{91}{216}$. The total chance of a loss, therefore, is $\frac{125}{216}$. There is a bonus to your effective chance given by the multiplying win, however. There's a $\frac{1}{216}$ chance of getting all 3, so one of your 91 wins is worth 3, not 1. Also, for 2 dice, you have three different ways of realising the chance $\frac{1}{6} * \frac{1}{6} * \frac{5}{6}$, because the losing die can come first, second or third. So that's another 15 chances out of your 91 that should be worth 2, not 1. So 91 + 15 + 2 is 108, and your chance of winning is $\frac{108}{233}$, or 0.46. Don't be fooled by 108 being half of 216 – those extra 17 we effectively added to counterbalance multiple wins add to the 216 total possibles too, because they are value weightings for certain results, not 'bonus' possibilities.

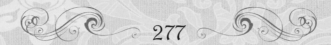HE ST. PATRICK'S DAY PARADE

Answer 144. The lowest common multiple of 2, 3, 4, 5, 6, 7, 8, 9 and 10 is 2,520, taking one from that would give you the lowest number that will leave 1 space after being divided by each of them. But 2,519 is divisible by 11, and we know from the question that the marchers are not. (2 * 2,520)-1 is not divisible by 11 however, so the number on the march is 5,039.

HE BOARDING HOUSE PIE

Answer 145.

DOMESTIC COMPLICATIONS

Answer 146. Mrs. Jones is Mr. Smith's daughter, and her mother's sister was Mr. Brown's wife, so there are only four people involved in the whole thing. The change at the end of the month is $8, or $2 each.

THE CONVENT

Answer 147. Before the soldiers came, there were 36 nuns, with 24 on the top floor and 12 on the bottom. The four corner rooms on each floor held 1 nun, whilst the four central rooms held 5 on the top floor and 2 on the bottom. Afterwards, there were 27 nuns left, 18 on the top and 9 on the bottom. On the bottom floor, each room held 1 nun apart from one of the central rooms, which held 2. On the top floor, the central rooms held 1 nun and the corner rooms held three, with two exceptions. On one side of the building adjacent to the side on which two nuns shared a room on the bottom floor, the central room of the top floor had two nuns. Additionally, the corner room touching the two sides of the building with just 1 nun in each central chamber had four nuns on the top floor. That way, the nuns managed to keep 11 on each side, with no empty rooms and twice as many on the top floor as on the bottom.

OLD BEACON TOWERS

Answer 148. The tower is diameter D 23.875 feet across, so its circumference (pi*D) is 75 feet. The stairs wind round four times, so if they all collapsed flat, they would represent 300 feet of staircase. The supports are 1 foot apart. Although that 1' is effectively sloping upwards, so is the ground they are on – so there is 1 step per foot, or 300 steps.

ASEY'S COW

Answer 149. The train travels two bridge lengths minus a foot whilst the cow runs half a bridge length less five feet. If the cow had taken the other direction, the train would have travelled three bridge lengths minus three inches whilst the cow ran half a bridge length plus 4 feet 9 inches. Adding the two together, we know the cow could run a whole bridge length less 3" whilst the train travels five bridge lengths minus 15" – 5 times the speed of the cow. The train's distance of two bridge lengths minus a foot would therefore be equal to 5 times the cow's distance if the cow was going at the same speed as the train, or 2.5 bridge lengths minus 25 feet. If $2B-1 = 2.5B - 25$, then $0.5B = 25 - 1$, so the bridge is 48 feet long.

OT CROSS BUNS

Answer 150. Loyd states that there can only be three boys and three girls, each receiving one two-a-penny and two three-a-penny buns. However, it should be fairly obvious that there could also be 14 children, each getting one half-penny bun each.

CYPHER DISPATCH PUZZLE

Answer 151. The text reads "The puzzle is this. Let us suppose that Charles is one third richer than Ellen. Then how much poorer is Ellen than Charles?" The answer is that effectively Ellen has 100% to Charles' 133%, or 75% to his 100%, and is therefore one quarter poorer.

THE FIGHTING FISHES OF SIAM

Answer 152. If each extra devil fish makes the group proportionately faster, then each fish joining a group of x reduces the time taken by 1/x. So the fifth fish will reduce the time by 1/4, from 180 seconds to 135 seconds, and so on. With this in mind, initially the devil fish will tackle the king fish 3 to 1, with the 13th fish aiding one group to a kill in 180 seconds whilst the others stalemate. The best strategy at this point, rather than all the now-free fish attacking one king fish, is for the fish to split up again, so that there are two king fish being worn down by 4 enemies, and one attacked by five. The five will kill their enemy in 135 seconds, during which time four will reduce a king fish to 25% health. Once the five are free, they again split up, tackling the king fish 7 and 6. Seven fish will kill an enemy in 90 seconds, but they only have 25% of that to go, so they take 22.5 seconds for their kill. In the meantime, the six, who would kill in 108 seconds, have done 20% further damage, give or take, to the last fish. That puts the survivor on just under 5% health, with all 13 attacking it. 13 fish will kill an enemy in 48.5 seconds, and therefore will do 5% damage in about 2.5 seconds. So the total time for the devil fish to win is 180 + 135 + 22.5 + 2.5 seconds, or 340 seconds. If the fish had taken the option of ganging up as much as possible on one enemy each time, they would have required 180 + 90 + 63 + 48.5 = 381.5 seconds.

THE GOLF PUZZLE

Answer 153. There are two constraints to solving this puzzle. One is obviously that you want each shot to be as long as possible, to minimise the number of shots. The other is that you have to be able to reach all of the holes. If you don't allow for doubling back, then the best answer is 75yds and 100yds, the highest numbers which together can reach all the options. They'll let you do the course in 31 shots. However, doubling back allows you to get some extra distance at the price of some backtracking. By making the shots 25yds different, you gain a 50yd spread for your direct shots. Try this with shots of 100yds and 125yds, and you can do the round in 28 shots. Loyd suggests that his readers have said that shots of 125yds and 150yds will let you do the round in 26, but actually that works out as 30 shots.

PUZZLING SCALES

Answer 154. Puzzling Scales. From (a) we know 1 top + 3 cubes = 12 marbles. From (b), we see 1 top = 1 cube + 8 marbles. If we add 3 cubes to each side of (b), we get 1 top + 3 cubes = 8 marbles + 4 cubes. The first half of this matches the first half of (a), so 8 marbles + 4 cubes = 12 marbles also, or 1 cube = 1 marble. From (b) then, 1 top = 9 marbles, which is what we need to balance (c).

 LEGAL PROBLEM

Answer 155. It may occur to you that for a man to have a widow, he must be dead, and therefore most definitely ineligible for marriage. However, that's not strictly true. The man may have married one woman, separated from her one way or another, and then re-married his first wife's sister. Then upon his death, his first marriage would have been to his widow's sister – and, obviously, perfectly legal.

 HE NECKLACE

Answer 156. There are 12 sections, and 12 small links on the ends of sections, so it might seem that the best answer is to use those 12 to join all the links together, for a total cost of $1.80. However, there are two small sections of chain with six small and four large links between them. If you open up those ten links, then you have ten pieces of chain left to close and ten open links to use. Four links at $0.20 and six at $0.15 come to $1.70.

THE BOXER PUZZLE

Answer 157. If p1 plays M-N, then p2 gets four boxes immediately and plays G-H. p1 can then take D-H or not, but either way can't avoid giving p2 a win. Opening L-P is the same, except p2's first run is 3 boxes. If p1 plays D-H or H-L, p2 will play the other, forcing p1 into giving p2 a 9-box run. The only move p1 can make is to play G-H. Then p2's best play is H-L, giving p1 a 4-box cascade, but there is nothing after that for p1 to do that will not give p2 a 5-box cascade.

THE PATROLMAN'S PUZZLE

Answer 158. One possible solution is as follows:

 URF PUZZLE

Answer 159. $3 on A gets $10 back, and $5 on B gets $11 back. So $33 on A, $50 on B and $27 on C would guarantee you a win of $110 – for an outlay of $110.

 STRONOMICAL PUZZLE

Answer 160.

 PATCH QUILT PUZZLE

Answer 161. Found 41? If not, you might like to keep on. Anyhow, according to Loyd, there are 15 more girls' names to be found – Jule, Lena, Dinah, Edna, Maud, Jennie, Minnie, Anna, Carry, Mary, Jane, Mae, Judy, Hannah and Eva. You can definitely be forgiven for not spotting "Jule" and "Carry" though! You could also have Amie, Ani, Andi, Nina, Hanne, Cyndi, Candi, Cyn, Ina, Mai, Macy, Mandi, Ena, Deanna, Diane, Diana, Raine, Rani, Randi, Uma, Jenni, Jenny, Janie, Jean, Leni, and Leann nowaday. Nancy makes 42.

 PRIMITIVE RAILROADING PROBLEM

Answer 162. Loyd's answer is as follows. Assume that the engine approaching from the right, R, has three carriages r1-r3, and the engine approaching from the left, L, has four carriages l1-l4. R pushes back far to the right, leaves r1-3, and moves onto the siding. L pulls l1-4 out to the right. R backs up, picks l4-1, and takes them to the left. L goes onto the siding. R backs up, joins l1 with r1, and pulls all seven to the left. R's driver now makes himself a cup of tea and settles down. L backs onto the track and the other carriages, and pulls r3, r2, r1 and l1 to the right. It reverses, and puts l1 on the siding, then backs the others to l2, with R still, on the left. L then backs on to l1, pulls it forward to the track, then reverses it back towards the left. Now in order we have L, l1, r3, r2, r1, l2, l3, l4, R. L pulls five cars to the right, and backs l2 onto the switch, pulls forward, backs the remaining 5 to the group on the right, pulls forward with l1, backs up to collect l2, pulls l1-2 right, and reverses them left onto the group, now L, l1, l2, r3, r2, r1, l3, l4, R. Then by repeating the manoeuvre by pulling six carriages and then seven, L can collect l1-4 behind it in original order. R, in turn, is left at the head of r1-r3, and the two trains can go on their way.

HE ROGUE'S LETTER

Answer 163. The cities, the names spread out between words, are Cleveland, Baltimore, Raleigh, Dallas, Omaha, Macon, Utica, Winona, Norwalk, Andover, Derby, York, Thebes, Reading, Rome, Early, Dayton, Lowell and Ellsworth.

HE SQUAREST GAME

Answer 164. Most of the numbers are multiples of 3, which will not combine to get you to 50. Only two are not, 25 and 19. Together they give you 44, and the 6 makes 50.

 SWARM OF GOOD BEES

Answer 165. The eight resolutions are "Be backward in nothing", "Be on hand", "Be wise", "Be independent" (B in D, pendant), "Be benign", "Be on time", "Be honest" and "Be underhand in nothing".

EARY WILLIE AND TIRED TIM

Answer 166. Loyd points out that at the first meeting, Willie has travelled 10 miles, and between them the two men have walked the entire distance between the two towns. By continuing on to the other town and back to meet again, the men must then have walked the distance three times, and by the same ratio, Willie has walked 30 miles. They meet again 12 miles from Pleasantville. So we know Willie has walked 10 miles from Joytown for certain outwards, 12 miles from Pleasantville back, and 30 in total. 30 miles - 10 - 12 leaves 8 miles, and all the miles since leaving Pleasantville are already known, so the 8 must have come after leaving the 10-mile Joytown marker. Therefore the distance is 18 miles.

ERRY'S PARADOX

Answer 167. The answer lies in the assumption that the original criteria do actually define an integer in the first place. 'Define' is a vague term, and the phrase "the smallest positive integer not definable in under 11 words" is itself imprecise, ambiguous, and therefore mathematically meaningless.

# CROSSWORD

Answer 168.

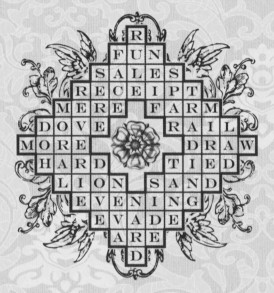

# THE HORSE PARADOX

Answer 169. The argument assumes that the groups you're breaking your horses into will always share the same single colour. That's true if you have groups which overlap each other, but when there are just two horses, divisible into two sets of one, the two subsets have no common horse. They are still sets of one colour of horse – they're just not the same colour. Without that foundation, you cannot say anything meaningful about any group of horses – except, perhaps, that they'll probably all like apples.

ASHING DAY

Answer 170. The answer is a towel.

ROPE AROUND THE EARTH

Answer 171. The counter-intuitive fact is that it makes no difference if the rope is around the Earth, a beachball, or the gassy outer shell of Jupiter. If you add 10m to the rope, you raise it by 10/2pi, or 1.59m. In other words, just 10m would be enough to raise the equator rope from ground level to chest-high all around the Earth.

 SCHRÖDINGER'S CAT

Answer 172. Schrödinger devised his cat as an illustration of how perverse quantum mechanics was getting. To his and Einstein's horror, it turned out that his original conclusion – that according to quantum mechanics, the cat would be both alive and dead simultaneously until someone looked, at which point its fate would resolve into one or the other – turns out to be an absolutely accurate illustration of way the universe works, as best we can tell. There are some different possible interpretations – maybe the box contains an infinite number of parallel dimensions, each containing one or the other possibility of the cat's state, for example – but the principle holds. Until a process is observed, it is in all possible states simultaneously. The Schrödinger's Cat principle has already been used to create communication streams that show, by their nature, if they have been observed or not. We live in a strange universe.

 HEMPEL'S RAVENS

Answer 173. Actually, the flaw lies in the reader's assumption that the proof has to be total. There is plenty of philosophical debate over the detailed implications of Hempel's Raven Paradox, but the bottom line is that if you see a green thing and it is not a raven, then that is at least a little extra evidence that there is no coloured thing that is a raven, and that therefore all ravens are black. The proof isn't absolute, by a long way, but it is proof.

WO TRAINS

Answer 174. The trains are moving at 50km/h and are 100 km apart, so they will crash in an hour. The fly is moving at 75 km/h, so it will travel 75km. Von Neumann however worked out how far it would travel to the first train, then how far back to the second, then back to the third, etc, summing up the series – all in his head, in an instant.

HE UNEXPECTED HANGING

Answer 175. The error is in assuming that Friday, once ruled out, has to stay ruled out. The prisoner is right that Friday would leave no room for doubt, and thus no surprise. But on previous days, there is still room for doubt. On Wednesday, the execution could still easily happen on Thursday, and so when it does happen on Wednesday, it is a surprise. In fact, if the prisoner believes his own logic, it will *always* be a surprise, negating his argument entirely – which really boils down to "I'm going to be hanged some time next week, which isn't surprising."

HE SULTAN'S DOWRY

Answer 176. The best approach is to reject daughters until a certain amount have been passed over, and then select the next daughter who's dowry is higher than that of the ones who have gone before. It turns out that the threshold point for this is at daughter number (n/e), where n is the total number of daughters, and e is Euler's Number, the mathematical constant 2.718... In this instance, the commoner should reject 37 daughters, which – coincidentally – leaves him with a 37% chance that the next girl who beats the ones before will be the one with the highest dowry.

FERMI'S PARADOX

Answer M. Fermi's paradox relies on a large set of assumptions, some or all of which might be false: (a) That we will recognise aliens or their activities when we see them. (b) That access to the Earth and its surrounding environment is unrestricted – we may be a 'zoo', in effect. (c) That aliens are not already here unofficially, or that governments would tell us if evidence was discovered. (d) That the Earth is sufficiently interesting to merit even the slightest alien attention. (e) That interested aliens could and would locate us in the vast gulfs of space if they actually wanted to in the first place. (f) That we have been looking for long enough – they may have come 500 years ago, for example. (g) That an alien civilisation is going to want to expand and explore in the first place. In other words, the unknowns are just too great. Fermi's paradox is a base for conjecture, but too narrow to provide any evidence for the non-existence of alien life.

THE PRISONER'S DILEMMA

Answer N8. Although the best collective option is to stay silent, the best individual option is to speak up. If prisoner B stays silent, then prisoner A gets six months for staying silent, and freedom for betraying B. If prisoner B betrays A, then A gets 10 years for staying silent, and five years for betraying B. Either way, A is better off if he betrays B, and betrayal is the best option. This only changes when both A and B can be certain of the other person's silence – which without communication, they cannot. It is encouraging to note that if the situation is repeated multiple times, so the prisoner knows what happened last turn, it turns out that the best strategy is to stay silent unless and until betrayed.

BOOK STACK

Answer 179. The number of books required to extend the stack a further book-length increases rapidly. For two books-worth of length, you'll need 31 books in the stack – and it takes 227 for a 3 book-length protrusion.

TWO ENVELOPE PROBLEM

Answer 180. The flaw here is in assuming that you can directly compare the situation where you lose half with the situation where you double. That's just not true. The two cases are different – the loss case assumes you have the higher envelope, and the win case assumes the lower. That means that they are not directly comparable. If you take the lowest sum as a constant when calculating your probabilities, you find that in either case, the risk calculation gives you an average of one and a half times the lower sum.

POSTAGE STAMP PROBLEM

Answer 181. The smallest unavailable number is 23. 1+4+7+10 is 22, and with no stamp just 1 higher than its nearest neighbour, there is no way to add another single digit to the sum. Because these stamps escalate in steps of 3, every earlier sum is reachable with the help of the '1' stamp.

STABLE MARRIAGE PROBLEM

Answer 182. Consider a man A and a woman Z. If A prefers Z to his current partner, he will have proposed to her first. If Z accepted, then the reason that they aren't married is that she preferred someone else. If she did not accept, she was already engaged to someone she preferred. Therefore it is impossible, using the Gale-Shapley algorithm, for a couple who prefer each other not to be together, and the situation is stable, albeit probably a little galling for the couples in the lower part of the matching order.

Quine's Paradox

Answer 183. There isn't really any way out of this one. Any reasonably meaningful language is going to allow for flat contradiction. You can argue that the accuracy or inaccuracy of the statement is impossible to define, but that's really just shifting the paradox to the side rather than actually solving it.

Suiri

Answer 184. Robert loves Crosswords and lives in Strathclyde, where he is a tailor. Bill loves Sudoku and lives in Essex, where he is a builder. John loves Numberlink and lives in Surrey, where he is a policeman. Ken loves Wordsearch and lives in Yorkshire, where he is a farmer. Martin loves Suiri and lives in Norfolk, where he is a driver.

THE BIRTHDAY PARADOX

Answer 185. Because any two people can share a birthday, the number of chances for a link increases rapidly as the group size expands. A group of just 23 people has a 50.7% chance of having two members with a common birthday. This rises to 99% chance at 57 people. For absolute certainty, you still need 366 people (or 367 if you allow Feb 29th birthdays).

HAKURO

Answer 186.

WORDSEARCH

Answer 187. Gilbat, Maki Kaji, Howie Garns, Art Wynne, Dudeney, Sam Loyd, Ahmes, Euclid, Zeno, Fibonacci, Leclerc, Silverman, Zu Shi Jie, Liu Hui, Hinton, Alcuin, Damoeta, Tartaglia, Mahaveerachaya, Archimedes, Abu Kamil, Diophantus, Euler, Epimenides, Polya, Russell, Carroll, Hilbert, VALIS, Fermi, Gardner, Singmaster, Frobenius, Bezzel, Von Neumann, Bhaskara, Flood, Dresher.

M	M	T	Z	A	I	E	H	E	A	G	A	R	D	N	E	R
A	D	O	A	R	U	S	S	E	L	L	L	I	U	H	U	I	A
N	E	L	I	T	A	B	L	I	G	E	E	L	E	H	A	O	D
A	L	F	C	T	R	E	B	L	I	H	G	H	F	V	U	T
S	P	U	U	R	E	N	E	I	H	V	S	A	N	I	H	E	L
N	O	L	C	O	O	E	G	T	E	R	E	T	N	B	I	E	U
R	L	L	L	M	B	H	A	S	K	A	R	A	O	N	A	D
A	Y	A	H	C	A	R	E	E	V	A	H	A	M	N	T	S	A
G	A	Z	D	E	D	H	O	N	C	E	W	T	U	A	O	M	I
E	P	D	I	L	D	E	L	S	I	A	Y	G	E	C	N	A	E
I	D	Y	O	L	M	A	S	E	K	U	R	E	N	C	N	O	E
W	A	E	P	I	M	E	N	D	E	S	R	N	E	N	U
O	F	P	H	T	I	N	K	J	P	E	F	O	E	S	L	C
H	E	C	A	G	Y	A	Z	I	M	L	N	L	V	I	D	L	L
F	R	E	N	W	J	G	E	H	S	E	R	D	O	N	U	I
A	M	E	T	I	O	R	A	S	Z	S	S	D	S	O	I	O	D
I	R	U	B	S	A	B	U	K	A	M	I	L	L	D	T	B
A	A	K	S	A	L	E	Z	Z	E	B	N	E	A	A	L	U	A

THE MONTY HALL PROBLEM

Answer 188. The common assumption is that as Monty has revealed a goat, the other two doors can hold either a goat or the car, so there is no advantage to switching. This is flat-out wrong. The truth is that Monty, by revealing one door, is effectively combining the other two doors into one option. If the car is behind B, he reveals C; if it is behind C, he reveals B. In either case, the car is behind the hidden door – that's two chances. The car being behind your door is just one chance, so if you switch, you have a ⅔ chance of getting the car. This is clearer if you imagine there are 101 doors, you pick one, and then Monty opens 99 he knows are duds to leave 1 other option. What's the chance you got the car right first time, versus the chance Monty has deliberately left the car hidden? The only time when it's not advantageous to switch is when Monty has no idea where the car is, and revealed the goat through sheer luck. Incidentally, after Selvin posed the problem, Monty wrote him a humorous letter in which he pointed out that in the real TV show, no switching is ever possible.

META TIC-TAC-TOE

Answer 189. There is in fact no way to know. Meta Tic-Tac-Toe is considerably more complex than the sum of its parts, and it is impossible to predict easily because of the varied strategic considerations. Give it a try, you may well be surprised.

SUDOKU

Answer 190.

NONOGRAM

Answer 191.

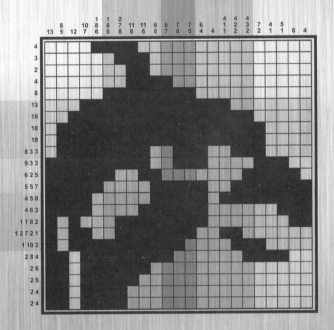

SUTHERLINK

Answer 192.

HASHIWOKAKERO

Answer 193.

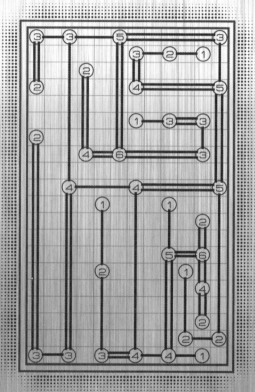

NUGGET NUMBER

Answer 194. The largest number that cannot be made is 43. Neither 43, 23 nor 3 are non-unit multiples of 3, and so cannot be made from 6 and 9. The six numbers from 44 to 49 can all be reached, and therefore any greater number can be reached (although not efficiently) by just adding further lots of 6 nuggets.

THE SIEVE OF CONWAY

Answer 195. There's no quick shortcut to this; you need to calculate each step, and it takes 19 steps in total. (1) 2 * 15/2=15. (2) 15 * 55/1=825. (3) 825 * 29/33 = 725. (4) 725 * 77/29 = 1925. (5) 1925 * 13/11 = 2275. (6) 2275 * 17/91 = 425. (7) 425 * 78/85 = 390. (8) 390 * 11/13 = 330. (9) 330 * 29/33 = 290. (10) 290 * 77/23 = 770. (11) 770 * 13/11 = 910. (12) 910 * 17/91 = 170. (13) 170 * 78/85 = 156. (14) 156 * 11/13 = 132. (15) 132 * 29/33 = 116. (16) 116 * 77/29 = 308. (17) 308 * 13/11 = 364. (18) 364 * 17/91 = 68. (19) 68 * 1/17 = 4. 4 = 2^2, and 2 is your prime. Phew.

GOKIGEN NANAME

Answer 196.

F ILLOMINO

Answer 197.

M ASYU

Answer 198.

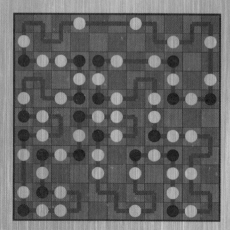

MAGIC SQUARE MATRIX

Answer 199. If you've managed it, congratulations; if not, the trick lies in taking the time to work out your template square. There isn't any quick way to do it, I'm afraid – but if it's any consolation, it's a lot faster than trying to work out a 6-order square without it. This method, which is the first discovered to date, is based on Willem Barink's 2006 physical puzzle game, Medjig. There are 1.8×10^{19} (that's 18 billion billion) 6-order squares, so giving one possible example seems redundant!

NUMBERLINK

Answer 200.